TED KOOSER & STEVE COX

Writing Brave and Free

Encouraging Words for People Who Want to Start Writing

UNIVERSITY OF NEBRASKA PRESS LINCOLN & LONDON

© 2006 by the Board of Regents
of the University of Nebraska

Library of Congress Cataloging-
in-Publication Data
Kooser, Ted.
Writing brave and free : encouraging
words for people who want to start
writing / Ted Kooser and Steve Cox.
p. cm.
Includes bibliographical references.
ISBN-13: 978-0-8032-2780-4 (cl. : alk. paper)
ISBN-10: 0-8032-2780-9 (cl. : alk. paper)
ISBN-13: 978-0-8032-7832-5 (pbk. : alk. paper)
ISBN-10: 0-8032-7832-2 (pbk. : alk. paper)
1. Authorship.   I. Cox, Steve, 1939– II. Title.
PN147.K69 2006   808'.02–dc22   2005020673

Write till you drop. Spend it all now.

Annie Dillard

CONTENTS

1. Writing Brave and Free 1
2. What's Standing in Your Way? 5

SECTION 1: Yes, You Can 7
3. What Do You Know? 9
4. Enchanting Details 11

SECTION 2: Rules? We Don' Need No Stinkin' Rules! 15
5. No Shoulds, No Should Nots 17
6. Input and Output 21

SECTION 3: Getting Started 25
7. The Ten-Minute Exercise 27
8. Overcoming Obstacles to Extended Writing 32
9. Developing the Habit of Writing 36
10. Don't Forget to Read! 41

SECTION 4: The Environment for Writing 43
11. The Writer's Tools 45
12. Your Clean, Well-Lighted Writing Place 49
13. Relax! The World Is Resting on Your Shoulders 51

SECTION 5: You and Your Readers 55
14. What Reader Do You Have in Mind? 57
15. Writing for Friends and Relations 60
16. Writing for Strangers 63
17. Taking Control 68
18. About Your Imaginary Reader 70

SECTION 6: Elements of a Piece of Writing 73

19. The Country of Memory 75

20. Writing about One Thing 79

21. Getting Organized 81

22. Sensory Detail 85

23. Suspense 88

24. The Size and Scope of Things 90

25. A Sentimental Journey 94

26. Transparency 96

27. The Unexpected Detail 98

28. It's a Figure of Speech 100

29. Before Us on the Table 105

30. Be Positive, Emphatic, Clear, and Active 108

31. Transformative Experience 111

SECTION 7: Revision and Getting Help 113

32. Revise and Wait 115

33. Getting Advice, Taking Criticism 118

SECTION 8: The Business of Writing 125

34. How Publishing Works 127

35. How to Get Published 132

36. Self-Publishing, Electronic Publishing,
    and Vanity Publishing 145

37. A Few Observations about Copyright 152

38. Fair Use 155

39. Obtaining Permission to Quote 158

40. Protecting Your Copyright 161

41. Conveying Rights: Contracts 162

42. Libel and Invasion of Privacy 166

SECTION 9: Acknowledgments and Further Reading 169

43. Acknowledgments 171

44. How to Write 172

45. Copyright, Libel, and Invasion of Privacy 176

WRITING BRAVE AND FREE

1   Writing Brave and Free

Carl Sandburg wrote poems all his life. When he was eighty-five years old, he published a book entitled *Honey and Salt* (1963) and in it is a long, free, funny poem about love.

In that poem, "Little Word, Little White Bird," Sandburg compares love with all sorts of lively things. Is love a cat, he asks, "with claws and wild mate screams in the black night?" Is love "a free glad spender, ready to spend to the limit, and then go head over heels in debt?" Or maybe, he says, love is an elephant, "and you step out of the way where the elephant comes trampling, tromping, traveling with big feet . . . immense and slow and easy."

Page after page, Sandburg slings ideas, comparisons, and images every which way, like a man digging through a box of favorite tools and pulling out this and that, pleased to show us what he's found. Never does he seem to doubt himself.

To write that exultant poem about love at eighty-five, Sandburg must have learned a way to start fresh all over again, every morning. He must have developed great confidence in his ability to write, and to write wild and free. Confidence is one of a writer's most valuable tools, and though it can sometimes be hard to find at the hardware store, we know where you can find it. We intend to show you that tool. It's right there inside you, believe it or not, hanging on a nail under the stairs, ready to be taken down and dusted off.

But first, a little about the writer's other tools.

Like Sandburg, every writer has a tool kit. Every writer needs tools you can touch and feel—a desk and a lamp, a computer or pen and paper—and tools you can't quite touch but can hold in your head— the ways to use nouns, verbs, ideas, metaphors, rhythms, attitudes, feelings, questions, memories of people and places, and the ways of organizing thoughts.

Most of the tools writers need they gather through experience.

Singers learn by listening to lots of music, and then by practicing and by singing in public. Writers build a writing tool kit by reading hungrily, by borrowing tools from other writers, by making a little time to write every day, and then by showing what they've written to someone else and carefully listening to what they have to say.

That business of reading hungrily and borrowing tools from other writers needs a little emphasis. Every writer learns by imitation, and the more you read, the more you find to imitate, to model your own work upon. If you want to start writing, part of the discipline is to read as much as you can. And you'll find that you learn almost as much from reading bad writing as from good. Each and every exposure to the written word will help you as a writer.

By the time he was eighty-five, Carl Sandburg's basic tool kit probably could have filled a freight car. Yet the most important things he pulled out of his kit every morning were his confidence, his joy in the work, and the heart to write wild and free.

The authors of this book are not yet eighty-five. But we're old enough to be retired from our day jobs (perhaps you are, too), and each of us has accumulated a garage full of writing tools.

Nobody else has had exactly the experiences you will be writing about. And nobody else has drawn on exactly our experience in writing a book about writing.

Ted has been writing and publishing for more than forty years. He has read his poems and essays to audiences in galleries, libraries, and sitting on the ground in a native prairie, and he has listened to writers read their own work in those same places. He has talked with and corresponded with other writers about their words and his own. He has led writers' groups and taught university seminars. Steve has written poems and essays and spent his working life as a book editor. Both of us have watched writers get started, and mature, and we've cheered them on as they have succeeded. We've both thought a lot about how to start writing, how to keep going, and what makes writing effective.

We've written this book for people who want to write and are looking for a way to get started—people who, halfway through a full life, want to set down what they know, people who may have some potential readers in mind, whether relatives, like-minded people, or complete strangers. We want to help people who have been saying for ten, twenty, or thirty years that they'd like to start writing, but who haven't started. Starting to write takes courage, of course, and maybe you've never been able to find that courage. We intend to help you find it.

We want to show you a few other tools—to tell you a few of the things we know, think, and feel about writing. Rather than offering a schoolbook that proceeds in a straight line from A to Z, covering all the bases, with quizzes at the ends of chapters, we decided to give you a short book resting on our own experience. We throw in a few surprises, some of them in unexpected places. You can skip around and open our book at any page and, we hope, get some good out of it.

We want to help you write because we believe there can never be too many writers. Why not a world in which everybody is writing? Surely writing, and the contemplative life that goes with it, is a much better way to spend your time than a hundred time-filling activities we could name. Besides, nothing is so exhilarating as to work at something you enjoy, and that's an experience that writing can give you.

Your own experience—the world as you live in it—is unique. It is a matchless, deep pleasure to write with love of your experience, to relive your life while you write it down, and to learn from your own experience as it unfolds on the page.

Your experience is unique, and so is that of every human being. That is one reason we want everyone to enjoy the privilege of writing.

Writing is not about showing how smart you are, says Barry Holstun Lopez, author of *River Notes* and *Arctic Dreams*. Writing, he says, is about telling the best story you know, the best way you can.

Writing both extends and makes permanent the sort of sharing we do each day. In everyday conversation, we tell each other anecdotes, we show others how to do things, we make up stories. Writing is no more than doing those same things on paper. It need not be intimidating. Writing doesn't use another language, but the language we're already using.

We know that the more regularly you write, the deeper the pleasure you'll take from it. We talk about the habits that help a writer get started and keep going. We've got our jumper cables handy.

Once you're in the habit of writing a little each day, we're eager to show you a little about how to develop as a writer, to show you some of the tools you can use to tune up what you've written, and we list a few books that explore the nooks and crannies of writing.

Lots of writers start by wanting nothing more than to express themselves—to write a poem that's a kind of primal scream that no one else may hear, a story that's like a tree falling in an unpopulated forest. We encourage you to go beyond that, to write to be read or heard. Perhaps what you have to say may be of real use to somebody. If you think about it, all day every day you're sharing what you've learned, what you know about everything from jacking up a car to making pan gravy. Writing makes a permanent record of that kind of sharing. It's an important part, even an essential part, of offering even your most common, everyday experiences to others in the human community.

We talk about how to attract and hold a reader's attention and how to make writing vivid and memorable.

If you want your writing to be read, you'll want to publish. We walk through the steps that can lead toward publication, and we give you a taste of the issues involved in copyright. But publishing is only a tool that helps you connect with readers. We're not trying to turn you into a successfully self-employed commercial writer—we believe that, for most writers, that's a false goal, an illusion.

Instead, we know only that if you sit down at the same time every day and—starting with a memory or with something you just saw out the window—you write for as long as you can set aside time for, at the end of even one week you will have produced something that you can feel good about. Isn't that enough? Even a few words a day is more than you had before you started. A novelist we know writes 250 words a day, day in and day out, and never tries for more than that. When he's finished for the day he treats himself to a game of computer golf. He has published a number of novels and several books of stories, just by letting those daily 250-word pieces add up toward something.

Why not say what we want? We want this book to be liberating.

We want to encourage you to ramble off on your own. We know you'll find a path that it would never occur to us to map. We ourselves have heard lots of advice, have tried many step-by-step regimens, and we know that the only advice that's always valid is "Get on with it!"

We're eager to see what road you take and, as you glance in the rearview mirror, we'll be there, grinning and clapping and cheering you on.

We wish you joy in the work and the heart to write brave and free.

2 What's Standing in Your Way?

How many times have you heard a friend say, "I think I've got a book in me" or "I think I'll write something about that." Maybe you've heard yourself say those same things. But when it comes to the writing, something goes wrong. You turn back from the starting line before the whistle blows and walk slump-shouldered back to the showers. You know what's out there ahead—the hard work of running the short sprint of a poem or the marathon of a novel—but you just can't set one foot in front of the other.

A big part of what's holding you back, we'd guess, is the fear of failure, the fear of losing the race to somebody bigger and faster, or the dread of taking on so much work. You want to be the very best writer ever, and you know you can't pull that off. You'll never get good enough to win the Nobel Prize. So you don't even try.

Well, aren't you setting your standards just a little high? You know you can't run a mile under four minutes, maybe not even under fifteen minutes, but that doesn't keep you from setting out on a nice long walk every morning. Writing can be like that, like a nice long walk, done at your own leisurely pace with no great goals in mind.

The poet William Stafford, when asked how a writer can avoid writer's block, said to lower your standards. It's some of the best advice we've ever heard. Sure, you can set goals, but make them reasonable. For example, you might set the goal of writing a description of the kitchen of a neighbor you visited often when you were a small child. A description doesn't have to have a plot like a story or a form like a poem. It's just a description, just a sketch. And yet it's something that is yours, something that you have written. Nobody else can ever write it the way you can, because it's coming out of your head, out of your memories, complete with details that nobody but you could include: the bent tin wooden match dispenser nailed to the wall next to the cellar door, for example. Or the five-gallon crock full of newspapers. And especially the curtained window looking out onto a garden that only you can remember in just this way. That sketch is enough. It's something. In fact, it's really something!

Little pieces of writing like that add up to bigger things. Every novel is merely a collection of scenes, written one by one and eventually arranged into a satisfying pattern. And lots of novelists say they start that way, by writing little scenes and by setting somebody in those scenes to see what they might do next. Lots of novelists write their books by following their characters from scene to scene to see how they react.

But that's fiction, and we don't want to push you toward fiction. We just want to get you writing, writing bits and pieces that *may* be parts of a novel one day, or parts of essays, or even just bright little passages in letters to dear friends.

But whatever destiny they may have, they're your writing, and only you could have written them in just that way. And hey, all of a sudden you've won something, haven't you? You've won a little blue ribbon and pinned it on yourself. It ain't the Nobel Prize or the Pulitzer, but you can be mighty pleased with it.

And for every one of those little pieces you add to the others you gain just a little confidence. Sitting down to write gets easier. If you have the confidence to give your neighbor your recipe for angel food cake, or to tell him how to start a stubborn snowblower, you have enough confidence to sketch out a little piece of writing.

SECTION ONE

Yes, You Can

3

"Write about what you know."

Writers hear that advice all the time. It sounds like an imperative, an order. It seems to draw a border around what you should write about, with a guard prohibiting you from stepping over the line into the realm of speculation or fantasy.

But the more you read, the more you see that there are no limits, no rules about writing. You can write whatever you feel like writing. You're free to choose, and that's one of the joys of writing. If you're painting, you can paint the sky green. If you want to, you can wear a red hat to breakfast. Did anybody ever tell you that?

Once when Steve was young, his Uncle Franklin accepted the job of babysitter and asked Steve what he'd like to eat. "A peanut butter and jelly sandwich," Steve said, and he asked, "Would it be all right to fold the bread over instead of cutting it?" Uncle Franklin was astonished. "You mean your mother doesn't let you fold the bread over?" To Steve's satisfaction, Franklin bravely broke the rule.

When you're writing, it's OK to fold the bread over.

There are rules everywhere. You have to stop at stoplights and take off your shoes at the airport and have money in the bank if you write a check. If you're a fry cook, you have to wear a hairnet, and your mother may have taught you that there's only one way to make pan gravy (some mothers say with a spoon, some with a fork).

But in writing there are no rules other than to remember that somebody's going to try to read what you've written and you don't want to discourage that person. Writing is communication, and it needs to communicate. Writing in a secret language you've invented isn't going to get you very far toward reaching an audience.

As to what you know, what you're going to write about, you know far more than you could ever write in a lifetime. The southern fiction writer Flannery O'Connor once said that by the time we're eight years old we already have enough material to last all our lives.

What you know arises directly from this very life you are living. It comes from your own experience, including the books you've read and what other people have told you.

What you know is more than facts—more than an old trunk packed with memories of people, places, and things. What you know is also how you feel about what you pull from that trunk.

What you know is also what you think about what you know. And, when you stop to think about it, isn't it also what you think about what you feel?

What you see, hear, touch, taste, smell is what you know.

What you feel—how your emotions move you—is what you know.

What you think, and what you imagine, about this world and all other worlds, is what you know.

That's what you're going to write about.

4

Do you worry that your life has been too ordinary to write about, that nothing of interest has happened to you?

A writer we know asked an old woman in a nursing home in Nebraska if she'd ever met anyone famous. "No," she said, and then, "Well, I did meet Lawrence Welk once. It was in the early spring, many years ago. It had snowed and the roads were all mud. One evening a car got stuck at the foot of our lane and a man came up to the house to see if Paul would pull the car out. It was Lawrence Welk and two members of his band. Mr. Welk said he'd send us ten dollars when they got to Sioux Falls, but he never did." This is a good little story, isn't it? And what makes it work are the specifics. Notice that she began with "One evening," which sets a specific time, and then she further specifies the experience by telling us the season and the weather. If you look at this anecdote you can see how it is enriched by specific details.

All too often we tend toward generalization. We say, "Well, the good old days were a lot better." Ho hum. We've all heard that, and nobody wants to read what they've already heard. When we read we're looking for unique experiences. If you find yourself falling into the Good Old Days mode of generalization, just ask yourself, Can I explain, using details, what made the good old days so good?

No life is ordinary once it has been written about using specific detail. The mere act of setting down your specific experiences makes your life uncommon and remarkable. When put into the right words, your unique life can become memorable, even enchanting.

If the house of your childhood was like every other house on the block, if your father had the same job as the fathers who were his neighbors, if your mother cooked and washed and watched over her children like every other mother, you might conclude that anything you write will be ordinary. But your mother and father, your house, what you ate and what you wore were *not* just like everyone else.

Let's say your house was indistinguishable from the rest of the houses on the block. The carpenter who built them had only one plan in his head—he didn't have to think about which room went where. There was a living room inside the front door, a dining room behind it, and a kitchen behind that. In the west wall of the dining room was a door onto a short hallway, and at either end of the hall was a small, dark bedroom. Between these was the bathroom, with the tub beneath a little window.

Every bathtub on the block was under the same little window. But it never occurred to your family that, because your house was just like the others, your family was like all the others. Mother could play the clarinet, perhaps, and Father knew how to make a dozen different animal shadows with his hands. There were nights when your house would be the only one on the block with the head of a donkey on the living room window shade, and that made your family different.

By carefully recording sensations, feelings, and ideas about the ordinary but specific details of life—a mother's clarinet playing, a father's shadow play—a writer can make the ordinary special, even enchanting. Remember that word—*details*—because paying attention to the details is essential to good writing.

Here's Alfred Kazin, remembering the vendors and all the foods of Brownsville, his Jewish neighborhood in Brooklyn, from his famous memoir, *A Walker in the City* (1951). He devotes unrelenting attention to detail and to the senses, especially to sight and smell—what he sensed, what he felt, and what he thought:

> Then in those late winter afternoons, when there was that deep grayness on the streets and that spicy smell from the open stands at dusk I was later to connect with my first great walks inside the New York crowd at the rush hour—then there would arise from behind the great flaming oil drums and the pushcarts loaded with their separate mounds of shoelaces, corsets, pots and pans, stockings, kosher kitchen soap, memorial candles in their wax-filled tumblers and glassware, "chiney" oranges, beet roots and soup greens, that deep and good odor of lox, of salami, of herrings and half-sour pickles, that told me I was truly home.
>
> As I went down Belmont Avenue, the copper-shining herrings

in the tall barrels made me think of the veneration of food in Brownsville families. . . .

We never had a chance to know what hunger meant. At home we nibbled all day long as a matter of course. On the block we gorged ourselves continually on "Nessels," Hersheys, gumdrops, polly seeds, nuts, chocolate-covered cherries, charlotte russe, and ice cream. A warm and sticky ooze ran through everything we touched; the street always smelled faintly like the candy wholesaler's windows on the way back from school. The hunger for sweets, jellies, and soda water raged in us like a disease; during the grimmest punchball game, in the middle of a fistfight, we would dash to the candy store to get down two-cent blocks of chocolate and "small"—three-cent— glasses of cherry soda. . . . At school during the recess hour Syrian vendors who all looked alike in their alpaca jackets and black velours hats came after us with their white enameled trays, from which we took *Halvah*, Turkish Delight, and three different kinds of greasy nut-brown pastry sticks. From the Jewish vendors, who went around the streets in every season wheeling their little tin stoves, we bought roasted potatoes either in the quarter or the half—the skins were hard as bark and still smelled of the smoke pouring out of the stoves. . . . But our greatest delight in all seasons was "delicatessen"—hot spiced corned beef, pastrami, rolled beef, hard salami, soft salami, chicken salami, bologna, frankfurter "specials" and the thinner, wrinkled hot dogs always taken with mustard and relish and sauerkraut, and whenever possible, to make the treat fully real, with potato salad, baked beans, and french fries which had been bubbling in the black wire fryer deep in the iron pot (Kazin, *A Walker in the City*, 31–34).

Wouldn't Kazin make any salami proud?

Notice the details. Those hot dogs aren't just hot dogs, but *wrinkled* hot dogs. You learn to write with detail like that by paying attention to the smallest things in your life. It's noticing those wrinkles in the hot dogs that makes your life different from the next person's, that makes your life unique and worthy of being written about. It's one thing to write, "Those winters long ago were severe." That's much too general. It's another thing to write, "One morning in January, 1936, Mother broke up the platform rocker she'd been given as a wedding gift and burned it in the kitchen stove."

Once you start writing, you'll be surprised by how many forgotten details surface. There's something about the process of putting words on paper that stirs up all the little things. Like one of those glass balls you shake and then watch the snowflakes fall back on the snowman. The snow is all the memories. You're the snowman.

SECTION TWO

Rules? We Don' Need No Stinkin' Rules!

5   No Shoulds, No Should Nots

Should you always write in complete sentences?

Should a poem rhyme? Should you always capitalize the first word in every line of a poem?

Should you end each chapter of a book by repeating what you just said and forecasting what you are going to say in the next chapter?

Should you always slavishly follow the rules of grammar? Elmore Leonard, author of *Get Shorty*, *Maximum Bob*, and many other admirable crime novels, says, "If it sounds like writing, I rewrite it. Or, if proper usage gets in the way, it may have to go. I can't allow what we learned in English to disrupt the sound and rhythm of the narrative."

Just so. We say that there are no shoulds, no should nots.

You don't even have to spell conventionally. Well, of course your reader may not understand your writing if your spelling is weird. Almost as important, your reader may stop and say, "What's this idiot doing? Can't he spell?" The most moving short story can be ruined by one little typographical error, because it immediately distracts a reader's attention from the story and raises a question about your ability to write. If you write clearly and conventionally, your writing becomes transparent, and your readers can enjoy it without having to stop and think about your mannerisms as a writer.

Many writers have been tempted to tell you everything they have learned about writing. When they do, they are likely to put those lessons in the form of a list of rules. Those lists seem delightfully contradictory. That's because when people try to distill all their wisdom about writing, they come out different places. Writing is a capacious activity that allows for a lot of individuality. Nobody's wrong, and nobody's necessarily right.

What you may take for rules are really just tools. Some are tools for communicating effectively and for helping readers to remember your writing. Others are vestiges of tool kits no longer in use. And there are tools that help you increase your—and your readers'—pleasure in the craft.

Your journal and your first drafts, which you write for yourself alone, can be as free as you wish. You sketch out your observations and ideas there, and they offer you the privacy to try out new ways of communicating. Then, when you are writing and revising to communicate with others, it's a courtesy and a good idea to use the tools at your command to help your readers as much as you can.

Accepted spelling and conventional grammar are tools that help your readers, and so does organizing your writing in such a way that it follows logic. Our first writing teachers taught us that every paragraph had a topic sentence and every theme had a beginning, middle, and conclusion. However boring and stodgy those lessons may have seemed, they were designed with clear communication in mind. Organizing your sentences into paragraphs and your paragraphs into an order that seems to be going in some direction is helpful to your readers and comforting, too. Writing—like painting, like music—attempts to create a little order from a largely disorderly world. The English mystery writer P. D. James said in a television interview that people enjoy reading mysteries because, at the end, when all the loose ends get tied, a reader senses that there really is order in the world.

Some tools that look like rules help your reader to remember what you have written. Take poetry for instance. Before there was reading or writing or printing, poets composed epic poems to be recited out loud and repeated word of mouth. Listeners could memorize the poem by the way it sounded. Rhyme, rhythm, and other patterns of sound helped the poem stay alive. What poems can you remember from your school days? More than likely they're the ones with regular rhythm and perhaps rhyme. Can you remember any poems that were written in free form? That's much more difficult.

You probably learned most of the popular songs you know the same way—by hearing them on the radio, not reading the words in a book. Because of their memorable sound effects, you may still be able to sing entire Cole Porter songs that you learned forty years ago. American country music in particular—where a bull's-eye rhyme for Texas ("all my exes live in Texas") is money in the bank—is passed around word of mouth, like old-time epic poetry. Unless you intend your reader to recite your writing out loud or memorize it, you may not want to bother with rhyme. (But poets might still consider writing poems that people can sing. The Scots singer Dougie McLean has set an old poem by Robert Burns, "A Slave's Lament," to music, and it's a showstopper.)

Just as rhyme is a reminder that poems were once written to be recited out loud, capitalizing the first word of every line of a poem is a vestige of old typesetting conventions—a device that in most writing has gone by the wayside. Nowadays you can feel free to capitalize the first word of every line of your poems if you wish to, or write in rhyme, or not. The thing to keep in mind is that your main object is surely to communicate. If rhyming and those capital letters don't help you to communicate what you want to say, then you can dispense with them.

At some point you may become intrigued with the craft of writing more than with the act of communicating—just as some potters quit worrying about whether a cup holds water and devote themselves to the craft of raku, in which it's OK to make pots that leak. If so, you may want to learn how to write particular forms—the particular structure of the sonnet that Shakespeare used, for example. Writing in strict form can be good exercise; it can be like working out in the gym to improve your tennis game.

Learning about traditional forms can heighten your awareness as a reader, which can find its fruition in what you write. After Steve was well along in college, he read a lovely poem by Philip Sydney. Steve had no idea why he loved it so much until somebody told him that it was a villanelle, a complicated form that can involve an accumulation of ear-catching repetition. When Steve read the poem out loud, he heard other alluring sound effects that, as a craftsman, Sydney had employed—all tools to win the heart of a reader.

Picking up new tools isn't all about becoming the next Shakespeare, either. The priest Andrew Greeley had a different ambition. He wanted to communicate his message to as many readers as he could, and he decided to add paperback novels to his tool kit of homilies, classroom lectures, academic treatises, and newspaper columns. So he sat down with a popular writer's novel that had been a best seller, and he wrote an outline of it, just the way you might have done in high school.

Using that proven model as a tool, Father Greeley has written dozens of novels that communicate his message to millions of readers.

Short of writing a formal outline, you can teach yourself quite a bit about writing by simply typing out a page or two from some book that you admire. It puts you in the writer's shoes, and you'll be surprised to see what tools the writer is using to make that writing effective.

The more you write, and the more you read with writing in mind, the more you will want to find the right tool for each writing job. And you may come to realize that the rule is simply a fact imposed by the Universe:

If you want to start writing you have to start.

The road is made by walking.

6 Input and Output

What do you write about, and what do you write about it? What you write about—call this input. What you write about it—call that output.

You are always drinking in the world. All writing begins with that—with your five senses. You write about what you see, hear, taste, smell, and touch. And effective writing begins with seeing the world clearly—so said the English poet and craftsman John Ruskin. "Hundreds of people can talk for one who can think," Ruskin said, "and thousands can think for one who can see."

You are bombarded every moment with sensations—the sight of a cereus blossom on your morning walk, the sound of a curve-billed thrasher's call nearby, the taste of tea lingering from breakfast, the smell of a creosote bush, the touch of a warm sweater on your arms—so many sensations that you may feel overwhelmed. Again, where do you begin?

The first step can be to focus on one sensation—to look, and to see one thing clearly, perhaps the cereus blossom.

That sensation—seeing clearly—is the first element of input.

Probably you singled out that one sensation because it aroused some feeling. What emotion did you feel? Joy, curiosity, terror, anxiety, calm, agitation? Maybe you felt joy, or a sense of loss of the wild world, or a love of the beauty of that perfect blossom.

What you feel about what you sense—that's the second element of input.

Then, what do you think about what you felt and saw? You sensed many things, you felt many feelings, and your thoughts about what you felt and sensed are quite complex, too. Perhaps you thought something complex about a city growing up in a desert that once was wild land, about how one perfect desert wildflower has thrived in the city.

What you sense, feel, and think—that's the input that you write about.

And, says our man Ruskin, "The greatest thing a human soul ever does in this world is to see something, and tell what it saw in a plain way."

In other words, when you write, you transform *input* into *output*.

Complementing the hierarchy of input—starting with sensations and proceeding through feelings to thoughts or ideas—there's a hierarchy of output that moves from information to knowledge to wisdom:

> Information—just the facts:
> On July 16, 2003, at Tucson International Airport, it rained one inch.

> Knowledge—organizing, summarizing, digesting an accumulation of information:
> The one-inch rain of July 16, 2003, was the first taste of monsoon season in Tucson, Arizona.

> Wisdom—an assessment of a body of knowledge, based on your own experience:
> Watching the sandy soil rapidly drink up the one inch of rain, I realized what a stranger I was in the desert. I remembered the rich, green, eternally wet forests of the Smoky Mountains, my true home.

This process of input and output is an endlessly repeated sequence of feedback loops, like those fractal patterns that repeat exactly the same form from the largest to the tiniest scale.

The process applies to revising what you have written as well as to writing the first draft. For example, what do you sense, feel, and think about the way you plan to organize your piece of writing? About the sentence you have just written? The word you have just chosen?

Sense, feel, think. Information, knowledge, wisdom. Keeping this process in mind will help you remember that you are writing out of your own experience. Your own wisdom.

> The one-inch rain of July 16, 2003, brought blooms to the "night blooming" cereus, a cactus of the Arizona desert. The cereus comes

in a variety of shapes—a cluster of little pincushions, a spider of green spiny arms, or a green sentinel of columns standing ramrod straight, chest high. The cereus does indeed bloom at night, but just as important, it buds and blooms only after the coming of rain.

Like other desert dwellers, the cereus waits through the dry spring and the hot, dry summer for the monsoons, the summer rains. It always seems that the monsoons will never come.

At first we see clouds, but no rain. Finally, the monsoons arrive in a gush, with an inch of rain on July 16, and early on the morning of July 20, the cereus erupt in bloom. Eighteen white satin blooms on a spidery plant, two pink blooms on the little pincushions, five more white blooms on the sentinel.

A woman contemplates the magenta blooms of a potted cereus and can't stop grinning. She has spent a lifetime learning, thinking, and writing about the healing power of desert plants, and for years she herself has been racked with arthritis. "I'm always full of pain," she says, "but when I see something so beautiful, the pain all goes away."

SECTION THREE

Getting Started

7   The Ten-Minute Exercise

Walk past a musician's studio, any time of the day or night, and you'll hear her practicing, endlessly repeating the scales and arpeggios that help her develop skill and grace on her instrument.

A painter's studio may be stacked with sketchbooks filled with rapid studies—exercises in capturing light and shadow, line and mass.

At a track meet, runners all over the field are stretching their tendons, flexing their muscles, warming up.

Writers practice, too. They fill notebooks with scribbling, write a whole book, throw it away and write the whole book again, and then set that draft aside and pick it up again and revise it, and then they write another one.

In other words, writing has less to do with possessing native talent and more to do with developing your ability through practice. Fortunately, getting started is easy: you sit down with a pen and paper, or in front of a computer, and write for at least ten minutes, just for the exercise.

If the idea of writing something seems intimidating, if like many people you are afraid it won't be any good, you might think of it as just making marks, the way our ancestors did, scratching on cave walls with charred sticks, which is what artists still do, whether they are drawing with pencils or making marks on a canvas with a paintbrush.

Making marks is the very best way to confront a blank piece of paper. It comes naturally to human beings, and you don't have to be a member of some special society to do it. Making marks is perfectly democratic. Everybody does it. It's not a question of whether they're *good* marks, just that they're marks on the paper.

When you sit down for your writing time, you might say to yourself, for ten minutes I'm just going to make some marks here. I'm not going to try to write anything *good*, I'm just going to make marks. And if the marks form letters, and the letters form words, and the words form sentences, and something good comes of making these marks, well, fine.

If you fill a notebook with marks, with words that interest you, with little impressions of things you've experienced, with random jottings of this and that, you'll soon discover something worth shaping into a more presentable piece. The process of marking will get you going. It really works.

At first, you're writing—making marks—for yourself alone. Writing memos, letters, and e-mail? No, that doesn't count. Ten minutes to write in your diary, or to write a poem, or a piece of an essay or story, whatever you want to call it. What you write in this ten-minute exercise doesn't matter.

You needn't write complete sentences or worry about grammar or spelling, and heaven knows you needn't stop when your ten minutes are up, although you may want to stop while you still have something to say. Ernest Hemingway said that he always stopped for the day at a place where he still had more to write. That way he had something to start with the next day.

Like the violinist's scales and the painter's sketches, what you write is an exercise, for your eyes alone.

The point of your ten-minute exercise is to develop the habit of writing:

- The habit of working with words, phrases, sentences, paragraphs.

- The habit of feeling the rhythm of words, of hearing your words in your ear, of seeing your words on paper.

- The habit of sinking into a subject, beyond the surface, into its own reality and what it means to you.

- The habit of thinking about the aim and scope of your writing.

Keeping a journal is like sharpening a pencil, says *New Yorker* writer Francine du Plessix Gray: "Our emotions, and the power of their expression, are kept at maximum intensity by the daily routine of being inserted into the journal's sharpening edge."

Alfred Kazin wrote his memoir of growing up in Jewish Brooklyn, *A Walker in the City*, only after having kept, all his life, "since boyhood, a voluminous daily journal, or sketchbook, into which went everything that I felt like describing and thinking about." Frank McCourt, author of *Angela's Ashes*, the grim memoir of growing up poor in Ireland, says, "the entire time I was growing up I was scribbling and reading."

Practicing will help you grasp the size, ambition, and subject of the poem, story, or book you want to write, and how much time it may take to complete, and what reader you are writing for.

What should you write? Where to begin? Here's your chance to write brave and free!

Your head is full of thoughts, observations, and stories you'd like to tell. The world is full of people, music, books, trees, and flowers to see, hear, touch, smell, and write about.

Since you can write about anything, you might start by describing something small and near at hand in intimate detail. You might describe your desk, or just the paperweight on it, or a rose in its vase. You might try to remember and write down a conversation you had this very day with a friend, a coworker, or a child.

And you can stop, if you wish, at the end of only ten minutes. Here's a ten-minute exercise Steve wrote one day, longhand:

> Monday was Martin Luther King Jr. Day and the kids were out of school and Carol Evans arranged for a bunch of us—twenty-five or so—from our church to take the bus to Mexico. Not just any bus, and not just any Mexico. It was the BorderLinks bus, and the driver was Lerry Chase, father of BorderLinks's founder, Rick Ufford-Chase, and the Mexico we went to visit was a border town, Nogales, Sonora, just across the U.S. line from Nogales, Arizona. Lerry took us through the big brown steel border fence made from landing mats from the Gulf War and through crowded downtown Nogales, up Obregon Street, busy with signs selling pharmaceuticals, music, furniture, clothing, all in Spanish—up the canyon that is the central feature of Nogales, and up into the dry dusty hills past cinderblock and wooden houses all crowded together, their yards completely occupied by old dusty cars and pickups, some of them running, many others that seemed not to have moved in ten years or more, higher up into the dry dusty hills. Finally he stopped the bus on a narrow dirt street and we walked up a steep hill, on a wide steep

> dirt and gravel path, to La Casa de la Misericordia, where Border-Links feeds lunch every day to three hundred schoolchildren from the colonias, the squatter settlements, on the surrounding hills—houses made of packing crates and tarpaper, then cinderblocks, and eventually electricity, clean water, and sanitation comes.

That's about 240 words, about one full typed page, double spaced. In ten minutes, some writers may write more, and some less.

However much you write, in ten minutes you can begin to sink your teeth into a subject, and you can begin to see how much more there is to say. In this exercise, Steve didn't even get to the good part—how the U.S. kids jumped right into a pickup game of soccer with the Mexican schoolkids; why thousands of people live in squatter settlements in Nogales; how that relates to the global economy, and what a surprising contrast Nogales is to Tucson, only sixty miles away; what exactly BorderLinks is.

Steve focused on physical detail. He dropped some hints about what he felt and what he thought, but in writing vividly about what you know, physical detail comes first. Writing from your imagination or your memories is fun, but paying attention to the details of daily life provides inexhaustible material. (And in September 2003, *UU World* magazine published an article that Steve derived from that entry in his journal.)

Each morning, Ted writes in a journal, and here's a representative ten minutes from him. He lives in Nebraska where the winters can be severe, and this entry was written early in January.

> It is supposed to be warm today, up into the fifties, very unusual for mid-January, when it can sometimes be twenty below. The sky this morning is a soft, warm blue with thin clouds drifting west to east.
>
> A warm day means that in the pasture across the road from us Todd Halle's cows and their yearling calves will be a little more adventurous and perhaps will amble toward the delicious-looking patch of pasture near our gate. Most of the winter they've stayed close to their water tank a hundred yards down the road, but the forage there has been trampled into the mud. The grass up our way is still tall and untrampled and surely they have been waiting for this kind of a day to take a leisurely stroll.

If they get too close, Alice may not be able to resist the temptation to try to get them running. She's got a little herd dog in her, possibly border collie, and it's just her nature to bark at cattle and dash under their feet. But that's a serious infraction in farming country, and dogs get shot for following their bliss.

One of our neighbors was a sucker for strays and had too many dogs to keep under control. On any given day he might have six or eight dogs he was feeding. He couldn't manage to keep the cow-chasing breeds out of the pasture across from his house, where his neighbor had a nice herd of Angus. Whenever one of his dogs got shot there was a familiar pattern of accompanying noises. First he would hear a rifle shot, the only sharp noise of the day, followed after a few minutes' pause by the sound of his neighbor's diesel tractor revving, and after a pause at the gate, turning into the pasture. Then he would hear the hydraulic creak of the loader bucket as it was lowered at the scene of the shooting, as the engine thrummed along at idle. No sound at all beneath the diesel whine as the dead dog was dumped in the loader bucket. Then there would be the hiss and creak of the bucket being lifted, another revving, then the gradually fading roar as the tractor and its bloody cargo rolled over the hill and into a grove.

My neighbor told me he never raised one word of objection because he knew the rules. And dogs were cheap to him.

But Alice is my only dog, and precious to me. So I need to decide whether to take the risk of leaving her free, or of feeling sorry for her all day for keeping her tied up or in the house while I am gone.

This exercise by Ted may never find its way into a more finished piece of writing, but he felt he had at least captured something worth noting.

With all the world to write about, you can see how hard it is to quit writing at ten minutes, once you've begun.

So begin! The next step is only a little harder: writing for at least ten minutes every day.

8   Overcoming Obstacles to Extended Writing

It can be fun to write for ten minutes one morning, and yet it can be daunting to face writing every morning over enough days, weeks, and months to produce something valuable or publishable.

One group of a dozen writers (nine women and three men, as we recall) listed these obstacles:

- Time
- Motivation
- Discipline
- Perfectionism
- Money
- Style
- Fear of failure
- Hating to write for all the above reasons

Here are some solutions that group came up with:

Time, that is, scheduling a regular time for writing every day. Make it a habit, like brushing your teeth, and over a period of several weeks it will find its place in your daily routine.

Motivation, in particular, not letting yourself become distracted by television, cats, the teapot, what's going on outside your window. Build in a reward, contingent on your doing your writing for the day, week, or month, with the size of the reward indexed to the size of the accomplishment. A square of chocolate for writing for ten minutes, a weekend off for writing every day for a month. As we mentioned earlier, one of our acquaintances rewards himself by playing computer golf.

Discipline. If you reinforce an activity with a system of rewards, gradually it becomes an ingrained, pleasurable habit, and that's all we really mean by discipline.

Perfectionism. Freewriting in first drafts—writing as fast as you can, without worrying about spelling or writing in complete sentences—can turn your attention away from trying to be perfect. Another effective tactic is, as William Stafford said, simply to lower your standards.

Money. Ask yourself, Can I afford to spend the time writing? How much time do you spend now in activities that don't bring home the bacon? Six hours a day, perhaps? Can you turn some of those minutes or hours into writing time without losing any income? A fiction writer we know, who has a regular eight-hour job, goes to a coffeehouse each noon and sits at the back and writes as she eats her lunch.

Style. Maybe your style of writing doesn't fit the style of the magazines in which you want to publish. When you're writing, you can write however you wish, but publishing may require making compromises. You may have to alter your style to fit the magazine. It may be a better choice to seek out magazines that seem to be using writing like yours. Donald Barthelme's surrealistic short stories changed the style of the *New Yorker*, but you shouldn't count on something like that happening in your favor.

Fear of failure. Build rejection into your expectations: plan to have magazines reject your writing, and treat it as a gift when you get published. As hard as it is to accept, every failure is a chance to learn.

Ted has found this useful: When something he's written is rejected, he says aloud to that distant editor, "Well, you know, I did the best I could. If I could've written it better, I would have." If you do the best you can, it may not be what somebody wants to publish, but you've done the best you can for that time and that stage of your development as a writer. And you'll get better the more you try!

Hating to write for all the above reasons. If you reward yourself for tackling one or two of the biggest obstacles you face, or if you focus first on the things about writing that you like, you may find that your other reservations fade away. One person who voiced this objection found that freewriting eased her mind and made her a more contented writer. It seemed that perfectionism was her biggest obstacle.

Robert Boice, a professor who helps other professors with their writing, studied the "self-talk" of a group of forty blocked writers. Here are the seven things they said to themselves that kept them from writing. We've given our responses, leaning on one of our favorite teachers of writing, Brenda Ueland:

1. *Writing is too fatiguing and unpleasant; almost anything else would be more fun.* Brenda Ueland exhorts her students with every fiber of her being to take a more positive tack. "Know that it is good to work. Work with love and think of liking it when you do it. It is easy and interesting. It is a privilege. There is nothing hard about it but your anxious vanity and fear of failure."

2. *It's OK to put writing off, to procrastinate.* Somebody taught us, and we believe it, that refusing to decide is itself a decision. Deciding to procrastinate is deciding not to write. It's also a positive decision to do whatever you do when you put off writing. Maybe you decide to take a shower instead, or go listen to Lucinda Williams, and those can be excellent choices, but they're not writing.

3. *I'm not in the mood to write; I'm too depressed or unmotivated to write.* The prolific novelist William Faulkner said, "I write when the spirit moves me. And the spirit moves me every day."

4. *I feel impatient about writing; I need to rush to catch up on all the projects that I should already have finished.* Right problem but, we say, wrong solution. On the one hand, every writer has many projects in mind or outlined or at some stage of research or contemplation. But sitting at her desk, a writer can only set down one word at a time, can only write the one poem or story or article that is before her.

5. *My writing must be mistake-free and better than the usual stuff that gets published.* If you say this to yourself, the legendary writing teacher Brenda Ueland has got your number: "Don't always be appraising yourself, wondering if you are better or worse than other writers. . . . Since you are like no other being ever created since the beginning of Time, you are incomparable." Glib writers who are satisfied with their work are the unfortunate ones, she says. "To them, the ocean is only knee-deep."

6. *My writing will probably be criticized and I may feel humiliated.* Brenda Ueland says this attitude arises from a lack of self-respect, not from modesty—she says that women especially are "too ready not to stand by what we have said or done. . . . It is so conceited and timid to be ashamed of one's mistakes. Of course they are mistakes. Go on to the next."

7. *Good writing is done in a single draft, preferably in a long session.* Every writer knows that the opposite is true. It is done in many briefer sessions, and every writer goes through many drafts to arrive at the finished piece.

Buried beneath all these obstacles, so deep that many people can't even express it, is an elemental fear that goes something like this:

When I write, I expose myself, and that makes me afraid. Yes. How does anyone overcome a fear? By experience, it seems to us. You write and find that nothing bad comes of it. And you always control and have the right to control what you expose about yourself in your writing. You may never overcome that fear completely, but you may overwhelm it with the joyful and contented habit of writing every day.

9   Developing the Habit of Writing

You get up and do your morning stretches. You bathe, maybe you shave your face or your legs. You get dressed, eat breakfast, take your meds, brush and floss your teeth.

You probably know by heart a list of essential good daily habits: Get some exercise. Eat lots of fruits and vegetables. Spend time with other people.

Everybody has to get up, get dressed, and go to work, whether they are retired or not, a doctor once told Steve. This doctor said that everybody ought to sit down to eat three meals a day (eating a Krispy Kreme doughnut behind the wheel doesn't count as breakfast) and everybody ought to put on sunscreen (this doctor was a dermatologist) before going out in the midday sun.

Good or bad, habits are the routines that carry over from one day to the next like the heavy flywheel that, by spinning steadily, evens out the staccato power strokes of an engine and keeps it running smoothly over the long haul.

Beginning writers sometimes say, "Well, I've written the first three paragraphs of what I want to write, but I'm stuck writing the fourth paragraph."

Writing every day can help get you over that hump. What you write tomorrow may not be the fourth paragraph you are seeking, but writing daily will keep you writing something, even when it seems that fourth paragraph won't come.

Once you're in the habit, the writing itself becomes the flywheel. If you're an artist making a drawing from life, there comes a moment of transition, says the British writer John Berger, when the artist loses interest in the subject and becomes interested in the drawing. That happens in daily writing, too: writing regularly, every day, you become absorbed, not in your subject, but in the writing itself.

For writers, the one essential habit is writing every day. And it's got three advantages over brushing your teeth:

- You're working hard at your writing for the pure joy of it, as Stephen King says—because you want to, not because a doctor or the spirit of your mother told you to.
- Writing is a lot more fun than brushing your teeth.
- Brushing your teeth is pure process; all you have to show for it in the short haul is a mouth tasting of toothpaste. Writing daily is a process, too, but the result is a product—every single day you've got another entry in your journal. Instant gratification!

You may be thinking, Not another habit! I can't find even ten minutes to write every day! I'm already booked solid!

Will we be able to persuade you to schedule the time to develop the writing habit? And if so, how?

Should we shout at you? That's what worked for the future *New Yorker* writer Francine du Plessix Gray. After reading her "trash," her poetry teacher, Charles Olson, bellowed, "Girl, this is pure shit! You're going to do nothing but keep a journal for a year, an hour a day at a minimum!"

And she did. A year later she showed Olson her journal, and again he raged at her, shouting: "You're still writing conservative junk! If you want to be a writer keep it to a journal . . . AND DON'T TRY TO PUBLISH ANYTHING FOR TEN YEARS!" Again, Gray did exactly as she was told, and eleven years later, "precisely one year past the deadline Charles had set for me," she reports, the *New Yorker* published her first story.

No, we don't propose to shout at you, nor to reason with you (but haven't you already testified that you want to write?), nor to play the efficiency expert, dissecting your schedule for an unused ten minutes, nor to exhort you never to say you "can't find the time."

Long after Charles Olson bellowed at her, Francine du Plessix Gray came to appreciate the habit that he set out to instill in her. She reflected that he "did have a conception of craftsmanship. He said you go to work every day, you've got to write every day, and this daily activity of writing will sharpen your experience. . . . You picked up the journal habit from Olson."

You'll develop the habit of writing every day, not when you feel some external force pushing you, but when you feel it pulling you—when writing every day becomes seductive, irresistible.

What makes an activity irresistible? Wow. What about the right time, the right place, associations with past pleasures, availability, and the promise of a reward?

The right time: You need to find a time slot that is flexible, so that you don't have to quit when your ten minutes are up, and a time when you are fresh and can think spontaneously. We've tried writing the first thing in the morning, the last thing at night, when we sit down at our desks at work, when we're waiting for an appointment, the last thing before we leave work while we wait for the rush hour traffic to thin.

Steve remembers watching one writer on a boat trip through the Grand Canyon. She wrote in her journal at every available moment. She even wrote standing on the beach at the beginning of a river day; she closed her journal only when she had to step aboard the departing raft.

When do you want to enjoy the pleasure of sitting alone and writing?

The right place: Comfortable chair, a desk that doesn't wiggle and that has a clear space on it, good light, in a place that is quiet and private—those are some elements that would work for most people.

Where would you like to write? In bed, maybe? Or at a coffee bar?

Associations with past pleasures: That is, associations through the senses—sight, hearing, smell, taste, touch. A window onto a garden, choice pictures on the walls, favorite quiet music, a cup of tea, the odor of cinnamon or roses, the grain of a well-made oak desk, the smooth strokes of a good pen, the texture and color of fine writing paper.

What are the sights, sounds, odors, tastes, textures that you love?

Availability: Your writing place needs to be readily accessible when you want to write, and your pen and paper or computer need to be near at hand, too.

What writing spot is handiest for you?

Pregnant and sleepless, Barbara Kingsolver wrote her first novel, *The Bean Trees*, late at night in a closet.

Mark Twain wrote with a typewriter—a brand-new invention at the time—in a gazebo.

Most of us prefer some semblance of the comforts of home.

Steve once loved to write at the kitchen counter of a little stone house in Flagstaff, Arizona, in the early morning when everyone else was asleep. An efficient wood stove kept the room warm, the teapot was at hand, there was plentiful natural light from windows in two walls, and the kitchen stool was the right height for the kitchen counter.

In a one-bedroom apartment when he was newly married, Ted made a writing spot by dragging a cardboard refrigerator box into a corner of the bedroom that he climbed into to write.

A writer we heard of would put her two toddlers into a playpen, but they did so much yelling she couldn't write. So she took the kids out and let them run around while she climbed in the playpen with her typewriter.

Traveling people may well give up on trying to write in a hotel room. The chairs are too low for the desks, the air is superarid and either too cold or too hot, the light can rarely be adapted conveniently to writing, the art on the walls is without merit, and (unless you bring your own iPod) it's difficult to find the music you love in a hotel room in a strange city. You're left with nothing but your imagination. Better to carry your notebook down to the lobby or to a Starbucks where something interesting might happen.

Steve remembers writing on the elbow-polished bar of the Red Dog Saloon in Juneau, Alaska, occupied by only one other determined drinker; in a coffee shop in Nashville; in a beach chair on the Middle Fork of the Salmon River in Idaho; at a Lewis and Clark campsite on the Missouri River in Montana. Ted wrote a poem in the dusty hayloft of a barn and another while sitting on a sun-warmed roof he was supposed to be shingling.

Take a vacation! The best advice Kenneth Atchity offers in his book *A Writer's Time* is this: set up a simple system of frequent and delectable rewards, including vacation time, for completing your writing assignments. A stroll around the garden when you've finished your first ten minutes of writing. Sunday off when you've written every day for a month. A weekend in the woods when you've completed a draft of your book.

Writers, like musicians, artists, runners, and knitters, have to be willing to practice.

Let us repeat, with emphasis, that what they write when they practice probably will never see the light of day.

A writer's journal can be ephemeral, like yesterday's newspapers blowing down the street or graffiti that workmen come along and paint over. But it does feel good to write as best you can even when you're writing in a journal, to shape your sentences, to try to capture something.

A writer's journal is like the nice cup of tea a cook will brew for herself before preparing dinner. The tea is not part of the dinner, but it helps the chef think about the amount, complexity, and flavor of what she's going to cook, and what pots and pans she'll need to use.

Because it's likely no one else will ever see it, the writer's journal is the very best place to practice writing brave and free!

10   Don't Forget to Read!

Reading usually precedes writing. And the impulse to write is almost always fired by reading. Reading, the love of reading is what makes you dream of becoming a writer.

Susan Sontag

Reading and writing go together and even compete. The novelist and book dealer Larry McMurtry says that the trouble with writing is that it cuts into his reading time.

The best way to learn the art of writing is to read as much as you can—poems, folk ballads, the Bible, historical novels, scary novels, essays, history, biographies, the newspaper, magazines, cookbooks.

As the writer Chuck Bowden says, every book has something of value in it. And any book may influence what you are writing in unexpected ways. It may trigger a memory, cause you to see things in a new way, show you a way to organize what you are writing, or best of all, introduce you to just the right word to describe your experience. A really dreadful book can teach you something; it can teach you how to avoid writing dreadfully.

Toni Morrison, Annie Dillard, Frank McCourt, and the other writers who contributed to William Zinsser's book *Inventing the Truth: The Art and Craft of Memoir* talk as much about what they've read as about how they write.

Writers learn to write by imitation, just as painters learn to paint by looking at paintings, woodsmen learn to chop down trees by watching an expert wield an ax, and blue-ribbon bakers learn the art of the apple pie in their mothers' kitchens.

Read anybody's first poem or story and you can tell there was a model for it. The writer got a sense of what makes a poem or story by reading somebody else's poem or story.

The more you read, the more models you find to learn from and to imitate, and the more accomplished your work becomes. Everything you've read and experimented with simmers down into a rich porridge all your own. And when you add your unique personality and character, presto! you've got your own style, as distinctive as a sound-print of your own (and no other) voice.

Stephen King reads widely, reads all the time. He has published stories in a literary style, and when he writes commercial horror fiction it is because that is the model he has chosen to follow.

A young man embarking on a search asked a wise older man what path he should take. The wise old man replied, "The path is made by walking."

Just so, the path is made by reading. When you set out intentionally to read in order to complement your writing, you'll soon realize how one book leads to another. The famous book you went to the library stacks to retrieve may lead you to the dazzling and neglected book shelved just next to it.

Of course, following our advice, you may wind up neglecting your writing and devote yourself to avid reading. That's OK, too.

And, when you have earned a vacation from writing, what better vacation than to pick up a good book?

SECTION FOUR

The Environment for Writing

Should you write longhand, putting pen directly to paper, or at a computer keyboard? Sometimes one, sometimes the other, if you have a choice.

Writing longhand is like walking. The opposable thumb you use to grasp a pen or pencil is as deeply human as your ability to walk upright.

Humans are also distinguished by a big brain full of the sensations, emotions, and ideas that we want to put down in writing.

Some people can use their big brains better when they are walking, or working physically, than when they are sitting still. It has something to do with stimulating the whole person—heart, guts, muscles, eyes, and ears, as well as the big brain. It has to do with calling up memories—as the muscles of athletes and musicians demonstrate, the body remembers what the mind forgets. It has something to do with integrating sensations, emotions, and ideas, which is what writers set out to do.

Writing longhand is a physical activity—maybe not as broad-scale as walking nor as aerobic as running a marathon, but you still use a lot of muscles pushing a pencil. It can tire you out. After an hour of writing you may feel as if you've been pushing a wheelbarrow for a whole day. And the feel of the pen in your hand, the sight and odor and touch of the paper, those tokens of the physical world engage your senses.

Writing longhand, slowly and steadily, also seems to keep in step with the pace of reflective thought. Shelby Foote wrote his massive, three-volume history of the Civil War with a hand-dipped pen. He said it helped him think about every word.

If writing longhand is like walking, then keyboarding at a computer is like driving a car. It involves almost no physical activity, and the only sensations are feeling the invariable, light touch of the keyboard and watching the monitor. And like any modern car, keyboarding can be very fast.

In terms of the number of words you write, though, the difference is not great. Whether you are writing longhand or keyboarding at the computer, you will probably be able to write about two hundred words of prose in ten minutes, if you don't pause to revise.

For daily practice such as writing in a journal, writing longhand seems the better choice. That's what a therapist found who had her clients keep journals. She wanted them to reflect on their feelings and actions in an orderly manner, and she determined that they dug deeper when they wrote longhand than when they wrote on the computer. Keyboarding, your fingers seem to race ahead of your mind. Or maybe they keep up with your mind without pausing for reflection.

It's in revising, whether on the fly or in later drafts, that the speed and flexibility of computers comes into play.

A computer is by far the tool of choice for writing and revising drafts of a piece meant for publication. (Even so, the smoothest results come if you ignore the cut-and-paste function and completely rekeyboard the final draft. The prize-winning writer Bil Gilbert observes that he can always spot an article that has been patched together on a computer.)

For many years Steve was a keyboard jockey eight hours a day, and when he got home from work he wrote longhand almost exclusively. He did it to restore some balance. The work of many Americans, from book designers to workers in paper mills, has changed from physical activity to sitting at a computer; they all need such a corrective to restore the relationship between physical effort and work.

For your daily exercise, and for your journal, we recommend writing longhand, in pen or pencil. For paper you can use a yellow legal pad, a Big Chief school tablet, or whatever paper comes to hand.

But consider: musicians practice on fine instruments, artists use good sketch paper, and even beginning surgeons use the finest scalpels money can buy. If writing is to be something you want to do every day, if it is to be irresistible, you might consider using irresistible tools.

Steve prefers blank books that are Smyth sewn, like a good hardbound book, so that they lie flat, with wide pages. He writes with a Fisher Space Pen that he can carry in his pants pocket all the time.

On a vacation in Tuscany, Steve's perceptive wife urged him to purchase a leather-bound blank book made of eggshell Florentine paper, and that was his daily journal until he filled it to the last page, both sides of every sheet.

Ted likes spiral-bound artists' sketchbooks. He prefers the spiral binding so that the pages lie flat. He likes inexpensive roller ball pens with black ink. He combines his journal with his fits and starts at writing poems, essays, and stories. That way, everything he writes is in one place. After typing a draft on his computer, he prints it out and pastes it into the sketchbook for study and revision.

Another possibility is to write on loose sheets of paper, punch holes in them, and keep your journal in a three-ring binder.

The choice of computers depends on what is available when the time comes to write on a keyboard.

Of course, pen and computer are only two of the writing tools available.

Bil Gilbert, who has been writing prize-winning articles for *Sports Illustrated*, *Smithsonian*, and other magazines since the 1950s, has always written on a typewriter. He has one supplier of typewriter ribbons, and he says that when that man goes out of business, he'll quit writing.

During the Typewriter Age, someone figured out that when people use typewriters, most of the strong words, the nouns and active verbs, wind up on the left side of the page. That's because moving the carriage return sets up a kind of regular rhythm—the writer pauses at the end of a line and attacks every new line afresh. The Beat novelist William Burroughs is said to have cut manuscripts down the middle. He discarded the right-hand half-pages, saved the stronger language on the left halves, and rewrote from there.

Computers, which wrap lines automatically, make for slack writing —we have to work toward stronger language on our own.

For the first draft of his splendid novel *Plainsong*, Kent Haruf set aside his computer, pulled a stocking cap over his eyes, and wrote blind on an old Royal manual typewriter. He said he wanted to regain the physical side of writing that you miss with a computer—the feel of writing on paper, the clatter of typewriter keys. He wrote blind, he said, in order to keep his first draft spontaneous—to avoid letting his analytical mind endlessly rewrite the draft sentence by sentence.

Haruf invented his blindness, but many people, such as Stephen Hawking, the best-selling author of *A Brief History of Time*, already possess physical limitations that they must overcome in order to write. Hawking, and many writers like him, are physically unable to write either longhand or at a keyboard. Fortunately, more and more useful tools, such as voice recognition software, have come into being to give us the opportunity to read about their sensations, emotions, and ideas.

Now that we've got you writing in your journal every day, you may be wondering whether you have chosen the most seductive, and the most ergonomically apt, place to write. Just in time, the next chapter is about your writing room.

12

Your Clean, Well-Lighted
Writing Place

When Kent Haruf wrote his novel *Plainsong* with a stocking cap over his eyes, he was working in a windowless basement room, formerly a coal bin, in his house near Carbondale, Illinois. When he removed his blinders, he could see around him, in his little writing room, objects that reminded him of the land far away, the High Plains of northeastern Colorado, where he set his books.

Haruf's story says that writing is more than thinking—it's also physical and emotional—and that you needn't arrive at your own way of writing by accident. You can choose a writing place and writing tools that encourage spontaneity and that engage your body as well as your mind.

Your writing room needs to be a place where you want to be, and it needs to give you privacy. It needs to be a place where you are physically comfortable, and a place where you can let your spontaneity bloom without interrupting or being interrupted by other people.

If you devoted one day's writing exercise to describing where you write now, what would you say?

What if you used a second day's exercise to write about what would improve it, the features you would like your ideal writing room to have?

Where Steve writes at home, he is surrounded by diversions, many of them pleasing—books, art, family, a beautiful British red tabby cat, a sunny window looking out on blue sky, citrus trees, and an adobe wall—and many of them unproductive distractions—the telephone, a barking dog, cookies. He has an old student's desk made of slabs of oak so thick that an earthquake wouldn't shake it. He has a Luxo desk lamp that provides a natural color of light. He rests his Macintosh PowerBook on a little writing table that he can adjust for height and angle. He sits in an inexpensive office chair with arms. He can adjust the arms, the back, and the height of the seat to make the chair fit his body ergonomically.

There are fewer distractions in his carrel at the university library. The walls are completely bare—the librarians do not allow you to hammer nails into the walls. The room is free of temptations: the telephone does not ring, the PowerBook is not hooked up to the Internet, and the librarians do not permit chocolate, cookies, or tea in the stacks. He can rest his eyes from focusing on the computer screen by strolling to the men's room.

Steve has brought to his carrel an adjustable table and a good light, like the ones at home, and has outfitted a solid, low library armchair with old sofa cushions and a portable back-support seat to make it ergonomically proper.

An overstuffed chair in the living room is Ted's favorite place to write, notebook on his knees, a cup of coffee at hand, his dog, Alice, at his feet. He writes very early, arising at 4:30 a.m. and working until 7:30 or 8:00. He likes working when his head is fresh from sleep and not yet cluttered with daily errands and obligations, and when the room is completely quiet. Easily distracted, he keeps the radio turned off, keeps the books he's reading out of his reach. He won't answer the phone while he's writing.

You need a writing place that doesn't inhibit your imagination and stimulates your creativity. Wherever you write, comfort is paramount.

You need to learn to relax.

13 Relax! The World is Resting on Your Shoulders

When you make tiny movements with your fingers to grasp a pencil or tap a keyboard, you bring your whole body to the task.

Try grasping your pencil in a vise grip. You can feel the muscles in your forearms tense up. And what about your posture at the keyboard? If you're sitting awkwardly, you can feel the strain in your back; when you stand up to go get a snack, you can feel it in your legs.

You need to learn to relax.

A well-known classical guitar teacher, Tom Patterson, starts by teaching relaxation. Professor Patterson says that, except during the brief moment when a finger is actually pressing and touching a string, the guitar player's whole body should be perfectly relaxed. He recalls the basketball player Michael Jordan. When Jordan wasn't engaged intensely in making a play, Patterson says, he showed perfect relaxation.

Like Tom Patterson and Michael Jordan, you'll do you your best work when you have learned to relax, and especially to relax your shoulders.

If your shoulders are tense, they quickly become painfully tired.

In their practice, students of Zen Buddhism sit for hours at a time. Relaxing their shoulders is one of the first things they must learn to do. In a retreat called *sesshin*, Zen students sit on their cushions from before dawn until long after sunset for seven days, pausing only for walking meditation. One participant, called the Tanto, is designated to carry a long, flat stick (the *kyosaku*) around the room and, with your permission, to whack you artfully on each shoulder with the kyosaku for the express purpose of helping you to relax.

A yogi drummer named Rex says that when he is playing a gig, he reminds himself, every ten or twelve beats, all night long, to relax his shoulders.

Just as with guitar, basketball, drumming, and life itself, writing engages both body and mind.

Human beings devote entire ways of life—meditation, psychotherapy, spirituality, hedonism, self-medication, watching television—to the mental side of relaxation.

The other half of relaxation is the body, and the essence of the physical part of relaxation is teaching your shoulders to relax.

Relaxation can start with good posture—erect, lower back slightly arched, elbows and forearms supported, elbows level horizontally with the work, so that your shoulders are not supporting any weight.

You may need to adjust your chair and your writing surface to make this possible. Some adjustments you can make cheaply, with a rolled-up hand towel supporting your wrists, for example, and a bath towel folded and draped vertically down the back of your chair to help keep your own back arched.

A physical therapist, massage therapist, or yoga teacher might help you improve your posture by analyzing and inexpensively improving your writing tools—the height and position of your chair, the support of your elbows and wrists, perhaps even the thickness of your pen.

Exercises for Writers

Writing involves making tiny motions with your fingers, with either a pen or a pencil or a keyboard—motions that engage not only your fingers' fine motor skills but also what physiologists call your large muscle groups—your forearms, biceps, shoulders, back, neck, and even your abdomen and buttocks.

Physical activity may help you to think. More than one person has said, "I don't know what I think until I write it down." Or if they want to have a talk that involves thinking clearly, some men (and perhaps some women, too) are more likely to say, "Let's take a walk," than "Let's sit down here for a little chat."

In contrast to longhand, writing at a keyboard can quickly lead to physical damage, especially if you use a mouse or thumbpad a lot, because you tend to use a few of your smallest fine muscles repeatedly and to neglect large muscle groups.

If you want to keyboard for another twenty or thirty years, it appears that you would be wise to use the keyboard instead of a fingerpad or mouse, rig up your workstation so that it's ergonomic, and stop keyboarding hell-for-leather by building in some pauses to stretch.

During those pauses, and even before sitting down at your desk, you might practice these exercises:

1. Curl your spine. From a standing position, curl your spine down slowly until your fingers touch your toes. Keep your knees bent and support your back by clenching the muscles in your butt. First, drop your chin, then your shoulders, and so forth until you are gazing at your thighs and your arms are dangling like ropes. Wobble your neck slowly and swing your arms lazily so that your fingertips are brushing the floor. Then uncurl slowly, again using your butt muscles for support, until you are upright. At the last moment you may feel your shoulders click into place like a well-crafted machine.

2. Ears to shoulders. Try to touch your ears with your shoulders, and then relax. Do that two or three times.

3. Shrug. With your arms dangling at your side, rotate your shoulders forward ten times and then back ten times.

4. Start the clock. Like a football official, stick your right arm straight up in the air and rotate it in a complete circle five times in one direction. Then go five times in the other direction. Do the same with your left arm.

5. The Elephant Nod. Drop your head slowly to the left, to the right, and forward, but not back—dropping it back may hurt your neck.

That simple shoulder-relaxing regimen takes less than ten minutes out of your writing day. And you can stop and run through it any time you feel like it.

Everyone agrees that walking is just about the best overall exercise known for human beings who are ambulatory. Brenda Ueland, in her books *If You Want to Write* and *Me*, emphasizes that long walks are important to her writing—to get recharged, to live in the moment, to clear a space so that ideas, "and even poetic feelings," could come. These creative thoughts come slowly, she says, like "silent, little inward bombs" of revelation that burst quietly, bringing "a feeling of happiness" similar to the feeling of learning a Mozart sonata at the piano. Brenda Ueland walked five or six miles, alone, and every day.

You can walk aerobically, as fast as you can, or you can choose a more contemplative walk.

In his book *Walking Meditation*, which has led many Americans to Zen Buddhism, Tich Naht Hahn urges you to walk slowly and to count your breaths in time to your paces as you walk. For example:

As you inhale: left, right, left

As you exhale: right, left, right

Zen encourages the student to count the breaths in groups of ten. In the above pattern, you would walk sixty paces for every ten breaths.

So: work at the keyboard ergonomically; don't neglect to write long-hand, too; relax your shoulders; practice the contemplative walk; and learn to relax!

SECTION FIVE

You and Your Readers

14   What Reader Do You Have in Mind?

"When you begin to write, have a reader in mind."

Writers have handed that old saw down from one generation to the next. But what good does it do to have a reader in mind?

Having a reader in mind means finding common ground with your reader. It helps you choose what—of the ten thousand people, places, things, thoughts, and feelings you know—to write about for that reader.

When she was in her sixties, Nora Foster wrote a little book as a gift to her granddaughters, the twins she had helped to raise. Nora was born in 1858 in a little town in Iowa, just ten years after the town was first settled.

For her granddaughters, Nora wrote about how it felt to sleep in a trundle bed beneath the rope bed that held her enormous parents—her father weighed almost 300 pounds, and her mother more than 240. When they would turn over, she said, the bed would squeak a tune.

Nora wrote about a great feast when her brother and his comrades returned from the Civil War. She wrote about music, flags, the deaths of a brother and sister, and about her own grandmother, who had helped raise her, sitting quietly and reading the Bible on the Sabbath.

Nora Foster wrote her little book for a readership of two, and to find common ground with those two grandchildren, she wrote what she remembered from her own childhood, when her eyes were wide open to a new world.

Some events—the Civil War, the Great Depression, 9/11—transfigure the whole world, and millions of people are hungry to read the stories of those who experienced them directly.

One such event occurred on Sunday morning, December 7, 1941, when Japanese fighter planes attacked the United States naval base at Pearl Harbor, Hawaii.

From the deck of a minesweeper, the USS *Oglala*, torpedoman Robert Hudson had an intimate view of the attack. He wrote a memoir that was published in a book of Pearl Harbor reminiscences. As Hudson remembered,

> a plane came directly at us . . . flying only about fifty feet above the water. Between the plane and the *Oglala* was a motor launch, returning people to their ships from liberty and church services. They looked up at the plane and all dove overboard. The launch raced on madly, without anyone in control. . . . The plane then dropped a torpedo straight for us. The plane's cockpit was open, and the pilot was hanging his head over the side to look at us. On his approach, we saw red flashes from his wings. I thought it was a drill and that the flashes were from a camera. . . . When bullets started ricocheting off the bulkhead around us, I knew the plane was not there to take our picture. . . . I ran to my battle station on the forecastle, a round chalk mark where a fifty-caliber machine gun was to be installed sometime in the future. . . . Men dashed about madly, crying and cursing. Planes were dropping torpedoes and bombs and strafing everything in sight. . . . I did exactly what I had been told to do. I stood on that goddamn chalk circle until ordered to do something else. . . . It was truly a nightmare to see shipmates . . . throwing potatoes and wrenches at low-flying planes (Paul Joseph Travers, *Eyewitness to Infamy: An Oral History of Pearl Harbor* [Lanham MD: Madison Books, 1991], 159–63).

Admirals, navy wives, and Japanese pilots, as well as sailors such as Robert Hudson, have written their memories of the attack on Pearl Harbor, each person writing what he or she knows.

No two of these reminiscences are exactly alike.

When you are writing for a large readership interested in one earthshaking event, as Robert Hudson was, having a reader in mind, and finding common ground, means thinking about what that reader already knows that you needn't say, and what that reader does not know.

Robert Hudson could assume that his reader, interested in Pearl Harbor, would know what a bulkhead, a minesweeper, a battle station, a fifty-caliber machine gun, a motor launch, and liberty are. He could use all those terms without explaining them.

What his reader did not know was exactly what Hudson saw, thought, and felt, and what he did. Standing in a chalk circle awaiting further orders and seeing sailors throwing potatoes at attacking planes—those are Hudson's own experiences, which his readers would want him to describe as vividly and intimately as he could.

What do you know that a perfect stranger will find compelling? You may never have been involved in an earth-shaking event, and yet a stranger may be intrigued by some arresting details of your life—the trundle bed, the sailors throwing potatoes at attacking airplanes—and it's in those telling details that you and the stranger find common ground.

How you evoke those experiences, what you feel and think about them, and how you express your thoughts and feelings, may also be the elements that keep your readers reading.

There are as many ways of telling a story as there are stories to tell, and your way will be unique. It's largely a matter of style, a matter of taste.

Dave Eggers achieved a sort of cockeyed fame with a memoir that stayed on the *New York Times* bestseller list for fourteen weeks and sold more than two hundred thousand copies, a book he had the temerity to call *A Heartbreaking Work of Staggering Genius*. It's a hard act to follow. Eggers's story is indeed heartbreaking. It's the story of how Eggers and his older brother and sister, all in their twenties, collaborated to raise their seven-year-old brother after their parents' sudden death. If Eggers has the license to call his book a work of staggering genius, it's because of the way he tells his story. What captures his readers' attention is what Eggers thinks, and how he feels, about his situation—and how he expresses his thoughts and feelings. By turns bitter and joyous, candid and disingenuous, Eggers takes his readers on a journey of grieving and of coming to terms with his life and his memories.

15   Writing for Friends and Relations

Do you long to tell your children or grandchildren about your own life, about the world as it was when you were young? Are you stumped about how to begin?

If you have been keeping a journal, writing for at least ten minutes a day, you are well begun. After even a week, you have already produced a record that your friends and relatives will find absorbing. But probably there is more to tell—much more.

What's got you stumped?

Are you worried about how to organize what you are writing? There's no need to worry at first. Keeping a journal, writing each day about one event or memory, you may be surprised at how quickly you will build a basic record. You can figure out how to organize the material later. Even when you're keeping a journal, many questions may stop you in your tracks.

Does your memory fail you? Can you not remember the name of that girl you played jacks with who wore the plaid jumper, or the year when you caught the record northern pike in Minnesota, or what you call that thingy on the side of an old clothes wringer?

When your memory fails you, there are three or four things you can do.

First, you can keep writing. More than likely the name or date will occur to you later.

Second, you can write around it. Describe playing jacks with the girl, or rowing the boat you were in when you caught the fish, or helping your mother with laundry, without using the name or date you are trying to remember. Or you can write about something else that you do remember.

Third, you can research. You can think about where you could find the information. You can check your own files or go to an encyclopedia. You can search the Internet. Or if there's a library handy, you can consult its inexhaustible supply of city directories, census records, topographical maps, histories.

Fourth, you could make it up.

We don't actually recommend that you make things up. But if you don't mind our asking, are you wondering how truthful to be?

Too many people write their memoirs out of the lowest of motives, to "set the record straight." Wanting posterity to think well of them, to forgive them, to dismiss allegations that they were out-and-out crooks, they lean toward making things up. But posterity is not as dumb as you might think. Posterity will figure out for itself when you are fudging. Whenever you try to set the record straight by bending the truth a little, posterity is likely to respond, "Baloney!"

We suggest that you tell the truth. If you write and publish a lie that injures a living person's reputation, that's called libel, and there are laws against libel. Telling a damaging truth can get you in almost as much trouble. As Stephen King says, when you step out to pick up the mail you don't want a neighbor taking a shot at you for something you wrote.

But really now, setting aside threats of lawsuits and violence, how truthful should you be?

What if you consider simple human kindness? Do you want Aunt Ginny to feel bad when she reads where you called her fat? Annie Dillard says, about writing her memoir, *An American Childhood*, "I tried to leave out anything that might trouble my family."

What you write about your friends and relations is also a question of tact, which has to do with good manners, which has to do with people getting along with each other.

That's one reason a private diary can be so fascinating—the writer is not considering the reaction of the reader, the feelings of others, the possibility of retribution, nor his own reputation. The writer dispenses with tact.

Professional writers can't always let mere tact hold them back. The novelist William Faulkner commented, perhaps tongue in cheek, that "'The Ode on a Grecian Urn' is worth any number of little old ladies."

Can you think of any books or poems that have been praised for their tact? Aren't writers more likely to be praised for their candor?

Too much tact is almost certainly the most common flaw of memoirs. However, telling the truth is also a matter of distinguishing fact from perception. "Writing in the first person," Annie Dillard cautions, "can trap the writer into airing grievances." Maybe you called Aunt Ginny fat because you remembered hating her wet kisses, while a more disinterested viewer—her family doctor, say—might describe her as just about the right weight for her age and height.

Ted once wrote a funny satirical poem about some people he worked with. When he read it to a friend, the friend said, "Don't be too hard on those people, Ted. You know, almost everybody is doing the best that they can." Ted stopped to think: does it really make sense to hurt somebody for the sake of one more stanza? Which is worth more, a person's feelings or a few cold sentences?

In writing as in life, there seem to be many ways of looking at the matter of tact and candor. Some writers act as if candor were the same thing as courage, others as if it were pure folly. Some writers act as if tact were simple common courtesy, others as if it were cowardice.

Writing about your life for your own friends and relatives, the main thing is to tell the truth. And if you can't tell the truth, either because you can't remember the facts or you don't wish to offend some living member of your community, well, you've seen the world and know a million stories. You can always just tell a different story, tell the truth about some other part of your life.

Maybe that's the place to focus—on telling the truth about what you perceive, feel, and think, telling the truth about your own life.

16

You're at an art opening—festive people, adventurous canapés, a strolling Stradivarius, a well-lit gallery, walls of intricate, colorful art—and standing next to you, gazing at the same painting, is a man you know you'd like to talk to.

He's a stranger, yet you feel you want to tell him something important. Maybe the painting reminds you of a week you spent in Tuscany, and you want to tell him how happy you were then.

How do you get his attention? In a room crowded with interesting people, full of fascinating art, how do you get him to listen to your story? How do you begin?

Probably your first step, the first step toward making a friend, is to put your listener at ease.

Writing for publication is like that. "Writing is telling a story to a stranger," says the writer Bil Gilbert. It's telling a story to someone you've never seen before and are unlikely to befriend, except through the printed page.

Even more than in that gallery, writing amounts to getting a stranger to listen to what you have to say. Your first task is to attract and hold somebody's attention. And your first step is to welcome your listener, to put that person at ease.

As you read writing you admire, notice the way it opens. Does it invite you in? Does it seem hospitable? Generally, writing is likely to engage readers the most when it approaches them with warmth and generosity, with both hands in the open.

John Crowe Ransom opens his poem "Vision by Sweetwater" this way:

> Go and ask Robin to bring the girls over
> To Sweetwater, said my Aunt; and that was why
> It was like a dream of ladies sweeping by
> The willows, clouds, deep meadowgrass, and river.

The first two lines are conversational, direct, matter-of-fact. There is nothing to obstruct or baffle or agitate Ransom's readers as they put their hands into the hand of the poet.

In the third line, having drawn his readers in, Ransom eases into more figurative language—"like a dream." You can feel the poem begin to accelerate, its wings lifting its readers off the ground.

In his poem "The Vacuum," Howard Nemerov uses only a line and a half to get his readers comfortably set:

> The house is so quiet now
> The vacuum cleaner sulks in the corner closet,
> Its bag limp as a stopped lung, its mouth
> Grinning into the floor, maybe at my
> Slovenly life, my dog-dead youth.

Once he gets to "sulks," everything changes; the vacuum takes on a personality, the poem turns fantastic before our eyes. But before that the language is plain and comfortable.

When, like Ransom and Nemerov, you speak to a stranger, the words you use are important. But so is your stance. In the gallery, it might be your body language, your smile, your nod of greeting that the stranger recognizes as friendly.

Writers can also put readers at ease by using a familiar storyteller's opening: "Once upon a time" or "It was a dark and stormy night." Readers know from experience that the writer is preparing them to listen to a story. The writer is asking readers for no other favor than to offer their attention.

James Herriott, the Scottish veterinarian, began his first book, the international best seller *All Creatures Great and Small*, this way:

> They didn't say anything about this in the books, I thought, as the snow blew in through the gaping doorway and settled on my naked back. I lay face down on the cobbled floor in a pool of nameless muck, my arm deep inside the straining cow, my feet scrabbling for a toe hold between the stones.

We know at once that we strangers are merely being asked to let him tell us his story, and we can settle in.

One way to put a stranger at ease is to talk about the weather.

"Is it hot enough for you?"

The heat of the noonday sun is something you both have in common and probably feel the same about.

Writers know the trick: It was a dark and stormy night. Everybody knows what a dark and stormy night looks like. Already, we're standing in the writer's shoes.

Herriott mentions snow in the first sentence of his book, and we know how cold snow would feel on a naked back.

Writers of personal letters often begin with the weather as a way of connecting with their reader—"It's been raining all night, and I have only a few minutes to write before Jill picks me up."

Weather leads easily to the whole setting of a piece of writing. The "weather" in Ransom's poem "Vision by Sweetwater" is the clouds and also the willows, the grass, and the flowing river. The quiet house in "The Vacuum" amounts to the same thing.

The object is to click, to express kinship with the reader, and talking about the weather is only one of many ways to do that.

In the tantalizing beginning of her memoir, Shirley Abbott uses image after image, like pulling rabbits out of a hat, to connect with her readers. She even includes her readers in the story with a deft use of "we" and "our."

> We all grew up with the weight of history on us. Our ancestors dwell in the attics of our brains as they do in the spiralling chains of knowledge hidden in every cell of our bodies. These spirits form our lives, and they may reveal themselves in mere trivialities—a quirk of speech, a way of folding a shirt. From the earliest days of my life, I encountered the past at every turn, in every season. Like any properly brought up Southern girl, I used to spend a lot of time in graveyards. On summer afternoons we'd pile into my mother's green Chevrolet—my Aunt Vera, her daughter June (four years my senior), and often some massive, aged female relative. Somehow we'd fit ourselves into the front and back seats, the women in print dresses and hairnets and no stockings, we two kids in shorts, and Mother would gun on down the road at 40 m.p.h. with every window open (Shirley Abbott, *Womenfolks, Growing Up Down South* [New Haven CT: Tricknor and Fields, 1983], 1).

Nor does Abbott neglect the weather, at the same time demonstrating the writers' workshop mantra to show, not tell. By her references to "no stockings," "kids in shorts," and "every window open," Abbott evokes the hot southern summer weather.

Ideas, cats, cars, crops, clothes, halfbacks, haircuts, and chrysanthemums all work just as well as the weather to connect a writer to one group of readers or another, so long as you're really talking about people, what they do and what they feel.

Same goes for leading off with the weather. The suspense novelist Elmore Leonard cautions that, unless you're writing about "a character's reaction to the weather, you don't want to go on too long. The reader is apt to leaf ahead looking for people."

Knowing your audience will help you find the right opening.

At a gallery opening, "Does her brushwork remind you of Mary Cassatt's?" may stand a better chance of getting the stranger's attention than "Hot enough for you?"

Whatever you say, when you meet a stranger, you don't want to seem to be trying too hard.

If there's one thing that can cause a stranger to turn away, a magazine to slip from a reader's hands, or a reader to close a book silently, it's pretentiousness, which means, loosely, trying too hard.

To capture and hold their readers' attention, newspaper writers learned long ago to scorn pretension—to get right to the story with a short, punchy leading sentence or lead (reporters spell the word "lede" to avoid confusion with the metal "lead").

One good lead can make a reporter's reputation.

Edna Buchanan, a police reporter for the *Miami Herald*, wrote one of the best-known leads in American journalism. It made her famous nationally and got her a book contract. She was wise enough to write the book the way she wrote her newspaper stories, and her publishers were wise enough to use her famous lead, the whole sentence, as the title of her book: *The Corpse Had a Familiar Face*.

Successful leads don't follow any rules except this one. Avoid pretentiousness.

Beginning writers sometimes think they ought to show their stuff by using big, intellectual-sounding, pretentious words. Maybe they think they'll impress the reader. Not likely, Buster. Generally speaking, a word that the reader does not understand is not worth using. Not in the lead.

And readers tend to skip anything that looks like literature rather than storytelling.

Elmore Leonard, who has written such satisfactorily fast-paced crime novels as *Get Shorty* and *Maximum Bob*, puts his money on telling a story, and not on writing literature: "Try to leave out the parts that readers tend to skip. . . . Think of what you skip reading a novel: thick paragraphs of prose you can see have too many words in them. What the writer is doing, he's writing, perpetrating hooptedoodle, perhaps taking another shot at the weather, or has gone into the character's head, and the reader either knows what the guy's thinking or doesn't care. I'll bet you don't skip dialogue."

17

Writing is telling a story to a stranger, but not to a stranger you can see. Not to a stranger you can grab by the wrist, lead to a park bench, and compel to listen as you pour forth your heart.

Whenever you write, you're preparing an experience for somebody else. But exactly how your writing affects that reader will be out of your hands.

Unless you recite at a poetry slam or sing your stories in a country bar, that reader will experience what you have written at some other time, perhaps after you're long gone, and in some far distant place.

Not only that, every reader is swayed by influences that the writer knows nothing about. Your reader may have come upon your story late in the evening, exhausted, or early in the morning, refreshed from sleep. Every reader has personal biases, too. The mere mention of motorcycles, cats, or Patsy Cline may turn one reader off and make another your lifelong fan.

The only controls you'll be able to exercise are the ones you build in as you write your story, choosing your words for the way you believe they'll influence your reader.

You have hundreds of opportunities to exercise control over the quality of your reader's experience. Every choice you make—even when you agonize over whether to use a period or a semicolon—can turn your reader's experience one way or the other.

For example, you can control your reader's experience by increasing or decreasing the difficulty of the reading. By increasing the difficulty, you slow the pace, encouraging your reader to savor a scene; by making the reading easier, you let your reader speed up. To convey the rapid punching, jabbing, and dancing action of a boxing match, you can use short, staccato sentences with lots of one-syllable words. On the other hand, William Faulkner's complex, "difficult" style slows readers down and may even suggest the sluggish, swampy, complex nature of his settings and themes.

But it takes a light hand on the throttle. A single difficult word or image can bring a reader to a complete halt, stopping the train altogether. On the other hand, language that is too simple can make your story seem like Thomas the Tank Engine to readers who are hoping for the Orient Express, or at least the Orange Blossom Special.

Beginning writers sometimes disdain controls. "I don't want to try to control the reader's response! This is a democracy! Every reader should be able to make what he or she wants from my story!"

On the contrary, writers in a democracy have a special obligation to write clearly and vigorously, not to play to an elite class by employing "difficult" writing. The longshoreman philosopher of the 1950s, Eric Hoffer, tackled big, troubling, difficult ideas in his books such as *The True Believer: Thoughts on the Nature of Mass Movements* (1951). His books rest on wide, deep, and no doubt difficult reading, but out of faith in common humanity, he worked hard to express his resulting ideas clearly and vigorously.

Writing of every kind is to some degree persuasive. Writers want to change their readers, whether to take some action or simply to see things from a new angle. To exercise that kind of control over their readers, writers must first exercise control over their writing.

Your distant reader may lose patience with writing that requires too much work. A vague, obscure poem can be heavy going and self-indulgent, and what the poet leaves out, the reader must supply. It can look to the reader like nothing more than sloppy writing. A reader is unlikely to take the time to make something worthwhile from writing that is mostly raw material.

Think of how you react to difficulties in your own reading. It's a safe bet that your readers will react to difficulties the same way.

Unless you are writing crossword puzzles, academic philosophy, high science, or tax law, your reader is unlikely to have the patience to labor over every page. Referring to the dictionary or encyclopedia can make reading more stimulating, but most readers, whether they read for pleasure or for edification, will lean toward writing that's clear and vigorous, and clarity and vigor come from exercising control.

18   About Your Imaginary Reader

In Samuel Taylor Coleridge's poem *The Rime of the Ancient Mariner*, a storyteller persuades a stranger, with better things to do, to step aside and listen to his tale. All writers work just as desperately to get their readers to pay attention.

The Ancient Mariner's listener resists because paying attention is work, too. But how hard can you expect your readers to work?

To answer that question, it's helpful to imagine a reader who is likely to want to meet you halfway.

Your imaginary reader may be someone predisposed to pay attention to your subject—a retired person if it's Social Security, a car nut if you're writing about Corvettes, a member of your family if your subject is Great-Grandma Nora.

It's harder to imagine the reader who will read what you write for the sheer compelling glory of your writing style, however delightful it may be to imagine such a lovely creature. Yet your style is what will keep your reader going, and as the poet Alexander Pope advised, it's only reasonable to meet your reader halfway by suiting your style to your readership.

Writing about a scientific topic for scientists, you need to use a more technical vocabulary than if you're explaining it to first graders.

Readers of the *New Yorker* may pause to read poems in a variety of forms, but if you expect to be accepted at the cowboy poets' gathering in Elko, Nevada, your poem had better march in strict meter, and it had better rhyme.

Your cowboy poem had better have some cows and horses on a vast sagebrush flat in it, too, whereas *New Yorker* poems tend to run to beach houses, great blue herons, and mollusks.

In addition to your subject (the cows, the beach house), and the form or style you use to write about it, your imaginary reader is likely to be drawn to your attitude toward your subject.

Cowboy poets and *New Yorker* poets both often take as their subjects life, death, nature, and love. An imaginary reader expects cowboy poets to take life earnestly but to find the humor in the human predicament—to laugh to keep from crying. The same imaginary reader may expect a *New Yorker* poet to express the anxiety that arises from daily living and then to go ahead and cry, or at least to fail to suppress a sob.

An imaginary reader may expect political opinions to be written in a state of highly charged cynicism, and fiction in the throes, as it were, of passion.

Who is the imaginary reader of what you are writing just now? A man or a woman? What age? How well educated? An American?

When you've finished conceiving your imaginary reader—someone you care about who might enjoy listening to you—you may find that you've imagined someone who is, in fact, much like you, with the same tastes, the same interests, and the same dislikes as you. Why? Because writers write things they like to read.

In creating an imaginary reader, it can help to think about the way you communicate with a person you know well, perhaps a member of your family. When you write a letter to your father, what do you leave out and what do you put in? Do you strive for accuracy? What about your language and questions of tact?

Imagining your reader leads to imagining where you will hope to publish your work, whether it's in a scientific journal, a daily newspaper, a general interest book, or a photocopied Christmas letter for your kids.

None of this is to say that you should always have your imaginary reader hanging over your shoulder. This can intimidate writers and get in the way of their originality and spontaneity.

But during the process of revision, an imaginary reader is essential. The imaginary reader can help you clean up and organize the raw material you have written down. You can ask yourself, are there places where my reader will have to pause and think? Do I really want to stop them there? Do I want to assume that my readers will be familiar with this experience, or do I need to explain it more? Is my imaginary reader beginning to yawn?

SECTION SIX

Elements of a Piece of Writing

19

The Country of Memory

There's more to memory than what you are able to remember of a time or a place at any given moment. Memory is multilayered, and beneath the most accessible layer you've stored away other, deeper layers, rich with detail.

From time to time each of us is suddenly surprised by some vivid memory that seems to come out of the blue. In the middle of an ordinary afternoon you suddenly recall the fragrance of freshly baked pumpkin cookies, with warm butterscotch icing. If you stop to think about it, if you stop to look around you, somewhere nearby is a little switch that turned that memory on. Perhaps it's the date on the calendar: maybe it's somebody's birthday, and you remember a party forty years before at which there were pumpkin cookies. Or perhaps you're swept back by the fragrance of the Butterfinger candy bar you just unwrapped for your afternoon snack.

Or, halfway through a sunny, productive day, you are suddenly weighed down by a ponderous sadness. Again it could be the date on the calendar: something awful happened on that day, forty or fifty years ago, though you had completely set that memory aside. Or the smell of cold bacon grease instantly carries you back to a kitchen in your past, on the rainy autumn morning your pretty young aunt announced to the family that she was going to die.

No doubt you can think of plenty of moments, much more affecting than these. The point is, the memory is richer and more complex than any of us realize, and there are triggers we all can use to reach the buried layers.

A number of years ago, Ted asked his late mother to describe the farmhouse in which she'd lived as a child. The house had burned in the 1930s, long before he was born, and he wanted to get a sense of where she and her family had lived. At first she was able to remember a few superficial things, the number of rooms, the way the house stood on the side of the road. Then he asked her to draw a floor plan of the main floor, the second floor, and the cellar. They got out pencil and paper and she went to work.

The process of drawing the rooms began to open the doors of her memory, and soon she was able to describe the patterns in the carpets, the position of the furniture, the pictures that hung on the walls. She was surprised and delighted at all she was able to remember. At one point, when she was drawing the upstairs plan, she said, "This is the room where Mama slept with us girls, Florence, Mabel, and I, and across the hall was the room where Dad slept with Alvah."

Ted said, "Your parents didn't sleep together?"

"Why," his mother said, "I guess not. You know, I've never thought about that. I suppose it was a kind of birth control!"

Another means of triggering memories is to go through old family papers, photo albums, scrapbooks, and let those picture and words take you back. Don't just glance at the people in the photographs, but take your time. Look into the detail in the background: the washboard leaning on the porch, the black dog asleep in a patch of light. Just what was that old dog's name, anyway, and didn't it kill some of the neighbor's guinea hens? And that neighbor, why sure, it was old Anna Muller, who lived in the summer kitchen after her son and his wife took over the house. She didn't bathe very often. Her son, Melvin, worked at the mill in Brockton before he took to drink and developed a swelling in his legs.

It's that detail you're looking for, the more the better. It's the detail that makes your writing vivid. Choose the most evocative details, the least expected ones. If old Mrs. Muller always had dirt under her fingernails, that one small observation can tell us more about her life than a paragraph describing her appearance from head to toe.

Your head is packed with those details—the Grand Canyon and the rolling sea off Cape Hatteras. Tons of colorful stone and slate-gray crashing water, the heavy tourist traffic, thousands of screaming gulls, and the frightened look your little daughter had on her face when you brought her first lobster and set it before her, claws and all.

The Big Bang theory has it that the whole Universe was once packed into a single, extremely dense speck. This is just the way the brain is, and everything you know and remember is inside the skull-sized speck that is your brain.

What any one of us remembers may not be as large as the Universe, but it would certainly fill a good-sized country.

Did your English teacher tell you that nouns are the names of people, places, and things? The details that you remember are, first of all, nouns.

Take just the people—never mind the places and things—that you remember. Think of all the people you know, your family, your friends, and all those who have died or have disappeared into the past. Stick to the ones whose names you remember, and flesh them out: If Jack Jones was six foot ten, stand him in your front yard at full height, and put the old woman with the walker right next to him, and your red-headed uncle and his red-headed kids standing at the curb. If you trot out each person whose name you can remember, short or tall, skinny or fat, you'll soon see that your front yard isn't going to contain them. They're blocking the street, trampling on Mr. Jones's freshly watered lawn. You're going to have to lead them to a bigger place—maybe the Wal-Mart parking lot. It's a parade, and every minute more people are pouring out of the side streets of your memory.

Then add places. Think about all the buildings you remember walking past, houses, stores, banks, filling stations. Reconstruct those buildings at full size, place them side by side, and add streets for them to front on. Maybe there's a park with churches on each corner, and shops along Main Street, and the water plant out by the dam. Add all the vistas you've surveyed—the broad, winding Mississippi from that park on the bluffs above Dubuque, the Sonoran desert, its saguaro cactus marching off into the distance, and the Sawtooth Mountains. Where can you put all those vistas? It's going to take a whole country to fit them in. The more you think of, the more memories there are.

People, places, and now things—the dress you wore to your junior prom, your first lace-up ice skates, the plush rabbit that your stepfather called Queen Victoria, your grandfather's milk cans that you pretended were horses, an apple crostada the way your wife bakes it, a rusty pair of Vise-Grip pliers your neighbor left clamped on an outdoor spigot.

Even a person who has never been to Europe or seen every state in the union needs a pretty big space for all the vistas, people, buildings, and things. Her country may be the size of Oklahoma, and yours could be bigger.

If you are open to a short safari into the country of memory, just fifteen minutes will give you enough things to write about to last all morning. And you can take along your thermos of coffee and your comfortable chair.

Those people, places, and things are rooted in your memory because of something the people did, and something that happened in those places, and something you or someone else did with those things. Every one of those nouns is attached in your memory to a verb.

When people get old and forgetful, we speak of their loss of short-term or long-term memory. As we understand it, short-term memory is like a to-do list. It retains activities that might matter quite a bit at the moment—some errand that needs to be run, some bill to be paid—but over the long course of a life, these minor activities aren't at all memorable and it's no wonder they're easy to forget. The file drawer of occurrences that carry some personal significance, however trivial they may have seemed at the time—that's what remains in long-term memory. How fortunate it is that long-term memory is the last to go. Your country of memory is always close within you, always open to exploration, and you have this for most of your lives.

Who says you have nothing to write about? You have a whole country!

20 Writing about One Thing

In your daily journal, you write about all kinds of disconnected things: the weather, gardening, children, motorcycles, cats, love, loss, life, death, music, Thanksgiving dinners.

Your journal may record the random events of your days, one after the other, or it may capture some of the random things roaming through your mind, none of them necessarily connected to the others.

When you tell a story to strangers, though, they will ask, What is this story about? They will expect the story, whether it's fiction, poetry, or a magazine article, and no matter how long and complex, to be about one main thing.

Your journal is like a garden of delectable ingredients to cook into your story. Like a chef planning a single dinner, you must find the one story you want to tell. You may not know at first what that story is. Most writers do not expect to make a story merely by transcribing journal entries. You may have to sit and let the story emerge as you stare at a blank sheet of paper or computer screen. Or you may just start writing. You may discover what you know in the process of writing. Writing brings people, places, and things to mind, and you discover your thoughts and feelings by articulating them.

Those of us who have a hard time figuring out what we feel about events, and then figuring out what we think about what we feel, may need to write several drafts in order to distill the answer, like the chef on the old television show *Northern Exposure* who, by constant simmering, reduced an entire steer into a single cup of potent sauce.

Frank McCourt says that he wrote journal after journal and draft after draft of his story, over many decades, before his best-selling *Angela's Ashes* finally emerged. Draft after draft, we approach the story sideways, a step at a time, hoping to gasp, finally, Oh! That's what this story is about!

If you record daily events in your journal, you allow the calendar to control what you write. If you record the things you think to write about each day, you let your memory have control.

To tell a story, you have to take control. Writing for strangers, you need to take control and shape your story. Your reading shows you that there are all kinds of ways to tell a story. It's such a mysterious, secret process that there aren't any secrets. Except that every story has a beginning, a middle, and an end. And that there has to be suspense.

And . . . and . . .

21

There are as many ways of organizing a piece of writing as there are writers and reasons for writing.

When an English teacher assigns sixth graders to write an English theme, they first have to turn in an outline that follows this form:

Introduction, stating a subject and a general idea about it.

Three examples supporting the general idea.

Conclusion saying, See, I told you so.

This exercise—like the philosopher's thesis, antithesis, and synthesis, and the more elaborate outlines you get in high school, and the schemes that teachers apply to Faulkner's short stories—is intended to train pupils in critical thinking, not to make them writers.

Of course, for some writers and some topics a formal outline is essential, and it may save time in the long run. The high school outline format,

I.
    A.
    B.
        i.
        ii.
            a.
            b.
                1.
                2.
    C.
II.

and so forth, tends to force a writer to be comprehensive.

A writer of technical manuals has to integrate information on all the components of the device she's describing. She starts with the smallest component and works her way up to the big picture, and she can't miss a trick. This is the kind of orderly, comprehensive writing for which the formal outline was devised.

Likewise, a scientist knows what path he must follow in writing proposals for research grants. He has to make an extended argument, a syllogism, proceeding step by step from where the reader is to where he wants the reader to wind up, while anticipating objections.

Writing a short article needn't require a very elaborate outline, but it may be useful to block it out in half-pages. If it's going to be six typed pages long, you've got only half a page to do this, half a page to do that, and then half a page to wrap it up. But many writers, once they've finished school, may kiss the formal outline goodbye.

At lunch one day, Steve asked four professional writers whether they wrote formal outlines before they began to write their articles and books. They all said no. Three of them, though, said that they were always terrified of getting started. They sharpened pencils, worried about housework, stared out the window, and finally sat down and just started writing.

For many writers, the chief benefit of an outline is to get the process of writing started. That's what Steve has found in his writing work-shops. He breaks the participants up into small groups and asks each group to spend ten minutes writing an outline using one of six styles. In four of the styles, including the formal outline, you draw a picture of the structure of what you plan to write. The other two styles hardly seem like outlines at all, and they are effective in a surprising way:

Freewriting an outline. You write as fast as you can, scribbling, using abbreviations and incomplete sentences, not worrying about spelling, capitalization, or any of the formalities. Writers find this method to be fun and productive, and it helps to give them a broad overview of their project.

They seem to cherish ten minutes when someone tells them they have nothing to do but write. One woman said she hated writing, which turned out to mean that she dreaded having to be perfect. Freewriting gave her the chance to relax and get started without worrying about perfection. At the end of ten minutes she seemed relaxed and happy, and she had something on paper.

Dictating to others. The person dictating gets to spin ideas out orally, without worrying about how they look on the page, and at the same time she gets advice from others in the group. Again, the person dictating has the luxury of talking out her project during ten minutes set aside for that purpose.

To get some ideas about organizing your own writing, you can reread books, stories, poems, or memoirs you admire to see how they are organized. As an example, here's a sort of free-flowing outline of one of the most admired of American memoirs, Alfred Kazin's *A Walker in the City*. Kazin chose an unconventional organization for this book. It's 176 pages long but divided into only four long chapters:

1. *From the Subway to the Synagogue*: A long, slow walk through Brownsville, the Jewish neighborhood of Brooklyn where Kazin grew up, from the subway stop that brings Kazin home from "the city" to the old wooden synagogue, only a block from where he was born. Drinking in the sights of the people, their activities, shops, and homes, and savoring all the food available on the street, and wondering about life outside Brownsville. Ending with Kazin's confirmation at the local synagogue at thirteen and his resentment of "this God of Israel": "He would never let me rest."

2. *The Kitchen*: The busy hub of Kazin's parents' apartment in Brownsville. The place that "held our lives together," where his mother prepared meals, where the family ate and observed Sabbath, where Kazin's mother sewed and conducted her business as a seamstress, and where Kazin slept in winter, wrapped in a blanket across two or three kitchen chairs before the stove. The place where neighbors and customers, "women in their housedresses sitting around the kitchen table waiting for a fitting," came in without knocking. "The kitchen gave a special character to our lives; my mother's character."

3. *The Block and Beyond*: The stores on Kazin's block and getting a taste of the world beyond Brownsville. School trips to the Botanic Garden next to the Brooklyn Museum. Seeing the whales in the Natural History Museum. First seeing the Egyptian and Greek art in the Metropolitan Museum, and then, in a dim alcove, paintings of Kazin's own city and Winslow Homers, Thomas Eakinses, John Sloans. Haunted by the blonde Mrs. Solovey, wife of the druggist on the corner, who looked exotic in Brownsville, had lived in Paris, and who came into the kitchen

and (the high point of the book) spoke French with high school student Kazin. At the end of the chapter, Mrs. Solovey, who knew the world outside and was a sort of exile in Brownsville, commits suicide.

4. *Summer: The Way to Highland Park*: At sixteen, with the encouragement of older boys and a teacher, Kazin the reader becomes a writer. He reads in the nearly empty library. He walks outside Brownsville to Highland Park and, with his first girlfriend, strolls around the reservoir and lies in the grass, looking "across the cemetery to the skyscrapers of Manhattan."

Kazin focuses on odors, tastes, sounds, and scenes and omits lots of details. Each paragraph and each chapter is free-flowing, and the overall organization is simple.

Dispatches, Michael Herr's gripping memoir of covering the Vietnam War, the book on which the movie *Apocalypse Now* was based, seems just as random in organization—260 pages but only six chapters, roughly chronological, each chapter filled with taut anecdotes and sketches, probably the best stories from his years as a correspondent. Herr made no pretense of knitting the stories together and separated one from the next only with an extra line of space.

22

Because vivid writing appeals to the reader's five senses, writers call upon vision, hearing, touch, taste, and smell both to set a scene and to bring a story to its conclusion.

Marilynne Robinson's novel *Housekeeping* (1980), the story of an orphan teenager named Ruthie, is packed with the things Ruthie sees, hears, touches, tastes, and smells, especially as the story draws to a close, when Ruthie and her Aunt Sylvie depart the town of Fingerbone, Idaho, by walking across the railroad bridge. "Nobody's ever done that," Sylvie says. "Crossed the bridge. Not that anybody knows of." And Ruthie relates:

> It was a dark and clouded night, but the tracks led to the lake like a broad path. Sylvie walked in front of me. We stepped on every other tie, although that made our stride uncomfortably long, because stepping on every tie made it uncomfortably short. But it was easy enough. I followed after Sylvie with slow, long, dancer's steps, and above us the stars, dim as dust in their Babylonian multitudes, pulled through the dark along the whorls of an enormous vortex— for that is what it is, I have seen it in pictures—were invisible, and the moon was long down. I could barely see Sylvie. I could barely see where I put my feet. Perhaps it was only the certainty that she was in front of me, and that I need only put my foot directly before me, that made me think I saw anything at all.
>
> "What if a train comes?" I asked.
>
> And she answered, "There's no train until morning."
>
> I could feel the bridge rising, and then suddenly a watery wind blew up my legs and billowed my coat, and more than that, there was a sliding and shimmering sound of the water, quiet sounds but wide—if you dive under water and stay down until your breath gives

out, when you come up in the air again, you hear space and distance. It was like that. A wave turned a stick or a stone on some black beach how many miles away, and I heard it at my ear. To be suddenly above the water was a giddy thing, an elation, and made me uncertain of my steps. . . . It was so dark there might have been no Sylvie ahead of me, and the bridge might have created itself under my foot as I walked, and vanished again behind me.

But I could hear the bridge. It was wooden, and it creaked. It leaned in the slow rhythm that moves things in water. The current pulled it south, and under my feet I could feel it drift south ever so slightly, and then right itself again. The rhythm seemed to be its own. It had nothing to do, as far as I could tell, with the steady rush of water toward the river. The slow creaking made me think of a park by the water where my mother used to take Lucille and me. It had a swing built of wood, as high as a scaffold and loose in all its joints, and when my mother pushed me the scaffold leaned after me, and creaked. That was where she sat me on her shoulders so that I could paddle my hands in the chestnut leaves, so cool, and that was the day we bought hamburgers at a white cart for supper and sat on a green bench by the seawall feeding all the bread to the seagulls and watching the ponderous ferries sail between sky and water so precisely the same electric blue that there was no horizon. The horns of the ferries made huge, delicate sounds, like cows lowing. They should have made a milky breath in the air. I thought they did, but that was just the sound lingering.

Ruthie strains to see in the dark night and imagines the sight of her own dancer's steps. She hears the creaking of the bridge and the turning of a pebble on a distant beach. She feels the touch of the wind billowing her coat and the swaying of the bridge. Then she remembers feeling and hearing a wooden swing leaning and creaking, touching cool leaves with her hands, seeing ferryboats sailing in bright electric blue light and hearing their horns, and she remembers thinking that their sound had the odor of milk.

Ruthie remembers confusing a sound with an odor. In another instance of synesthesia (stimulation of one of the five senses evoking perception in another sense), she speaks of the sound of water as if she were seeing its "sliding and shimmering." Her senses are so acute that they mingle together, yet she seems unable to name what she might feel most deeply.

Ruthie says that she feels giddy and elated, uncertain and afraid. But does Ruthie the orphan feel desperate, anxious, lonely, or angry? Robinson never says, and she has no need to. A writer doesn't have to come right out and tell the reader whether the speaker is happy or sad, if she carefully describes what's going on with the speaker's senses. The outer world—the swaying bridge, the creaking swing, the mooing ferryboat—becomes an integral part of the emotion the writer is setting out to evoke, rather than merely providing a fixed backdrop against which the action takes place.

23

What holds your reader's attention? What keeps your reader turning the pages? Suspense.

Even when it is a low level of suspense, more like calm anticipation, you want your reader to keep asking, how does Our Hero's situation get resolved?

It can be a simple thing—your reader may only wonder, how is this sentence about Our Hero going to end?

The situation can be stated very obviously—will Our Hero survive this climb up a vertical cliff? Or it can be more abstract, more hidden— what is the mystery about Our Hero that the writer hasn't yet told us?

Suspense needn't always be planned in advance, but can be introduced as you revise: Why don't I put off telling my reader whether it was Bernard who ran over the cat?

As you read, notice how writers sometimes set up suspense even in the first sentence. We can't resist reading on, to find out what happens next.

What can possibly happen after this opening sentence of Flannery O'Connor's novel *The Violent Bear It Away*?

> Francis Marion Tarwater's uncle had been dead for only half a day when the boy got too drunk to finish digging the grave and a Negro named Buford Munson, who had come to get a jug filled, had to finish it and drag the body from the breakfast table where it was sitting and bury it in a decent a Christian way, with the sign of its Savior at the head of the grave and enough dirt on top to keep the dogs from digging it up.

Or what about the more mundane mysteries packed into this brief sentence, with which D. M. Thomas opened his novel *Ararat*?

Sergei Rozanov had made an unnecessary journey from Moscow to Gorky, simply in order to sleep with a young blind woman.

Why was Rozanov's journey unnecessary? And why was it important to specify that the young woman was blind? Ernest Hemingway was famous for writing simple declarative sentences that somehow held his readers' attention. At first he seems to be dealing in flat, incontrovertible information. Eventually, some readers realize that what is gripping about Hemingway's writing is not what he says but the information he withholds. To create suspense, what you do is withhold information. You don't need a crime or a violent death in the lead to hook your reader, to get your reader to read on.

Like a lot of writers, we're keen on beginnings and endings—starting with a boffo lead, ending with a bang—but what about the middle? OK, the middle is everything between the lead and the concluding sentence, but still, what goes in the middle?

What if you think of writing as something like building a barn?

To order enough lumber to build a barn, you have to have a conception of how big you want the barn to be. To figure out anything about the middle of a piece of writing, you need to have an idea how big it has to be to do the job you have in mind.

But it's inefficient to build a barn bigger than it needs to be. So with writing: Your readers will be grateful if you can be brief. That means deciding before you begin writing how long the book, poem, or article will be. And it means cutting, as you revise, so that the completed manuscript is shorter than you intended it to be. You leave your readers hungry—tell them less than everything you know.

There are many ways to build a barn, big or little, wood or stone, rectangular or round, with or without a cellar and a haymow, and before you start it's also useful to know the shape of the barn you mean to build.

The barn you finally build may look nothing like the barn you had in mind, and likewise, your poem or story may not fit the form you started out with. Just as you budget the cost of the lumber for your barn, you might consider form as a kind of budget—"I'm going to budget fourteen lines for this poem"—even if the poem winds up being twenty lines or not a poem at all but a novel.

Here are some ideas about middles and forms:

Philosophers speak of the dialectical process, which provides a seductive model for writing because it has a beginning, a middle, and an end. You begin by stating a thesis ("this is true"). In the middle, you state its antithesis ("on the other hand, that is true"). And you end by stating a synthesis ("looked at another way, both this and that are true"). Expressed so baldly, it's a remarkably sterile form. The middle is nothing but objections, and the end is a kind of a compromise. But many poets have written with that dialectical process somewhere in mind.

Haikus are very short Japanese poems that reduce the world down to a kernel of acute observation. The classical Japanese haiku is a one-line poem of seventeen syllables broken down into three units—five syllables, seven syllables, five syllables. Some poets in English mimic the Japanese form in three lines totaling seventeen syllables, perhaps with the first twelve syllables setting a scene and the last five syllables making a comment on the scene.

Depending on how you look at it, the conventional form of a haiku may have a middle of seven syllables or no middle at all—just a beginning of twelve syllables and an end of five syllables. The most famous Japanese haiku, by Basho, who himself was the most famous Japanese writer of haikus, occupies seventeen syllables in Japanese, but in English can be translated neatly in just six syllables, six words:

> Old pond;
> frog jumps in
> Plop!

If you want to practice getting at the core of a sensation, feeling, or thought and want to write lots of poems very fast, haikus may serve you well.

If you're writing love poems, you may gravitate toward sonnets. A sonnet is a little song, long enough to express your feelings yet not so long as to bore the object of your affection. Shakespeare used sonnets to write about his thoughts on cosmic themes as well as his immediate feelings, and his sonnets are always fourteen lines long, rhymed in a fairly strict pattern. Sonnets of his day applied a sort of dialectical budget: thesis (six lines), antithesis (six lines), synthesis (two lines). Or the first eight lines stated a problem and the last six resolved it. Or the first four lines were the beginning, the next six were the middle, and the last four were the end. Or the first twelve lines were the beginning, the last two lines the ending, and there wasn't any middle. Shakespeare himself seemed to try to start off with a boffo lead, give lots of interesting details in the middle, and end his poems with a bang.

As we've mentioned again and again, one of the pleasures of writing is the craft of it, shaping your sensations, feelings, and thoughts into a form that readers will find pleasing, too. Writing in strict forms, such as that of the Shakespearean sonnet, can be very satisfying, and a good way to learn, too. Any piece of writing that you have enjoyed reading is likely to be a good deal more than merely a shapeless blob of self-indulgent meandering. The writer has put it in some form, although it may be more subtle than the rhymed sonnets that Shakespeare favored.

An epic poem is usually very long—so long that Alfred, Lord Tennyson never completed his, and Edmund Spenser scarcely got past the introduction of his epic, *The Faerie Queene*. An epic is the work of a lifetime, and if you're writing one you needn't worry about the middle or the end, because you're unlikely to get there.

A book, librarians say, is a piece of writing more than one hundred pages long. After reading the critical opinions of lots of book reviewers, the writer Randall Jarrell concluded that a novel is a long piece of fiction that has something wrong with it. Being books, novels have to be at least one hundred pages long. Beyond that, the sky is the limit, and it's even OK to make some mistakes.

Your imaginary reader or listener, and how you plan to publish your work, will certainly affect the size and scope of what you're writing.

Magazines nowadays want articles shorter than fifteen hundred words—that is, four and a half double-spaced pages in 11-point type. Readers today have a short attention span and magazines prefer to publish short pieces. (More important, short articles leave more space for the publisher to sell as ads.) A pundit's column on the editorial page of a newspaper runs about 750 words—less than two double-spaced pages in 11-point type.

Your published book, when set in type, will probably be shorter than your typed manuscript, but there are exceptions. A history book, that is, a book of serious prose, will usually be two-thirds the length of the typed manuscript. That is, a manuscript 320 pages long (double spaced) might make a book of about 212 pages. A romance novel, printed in larger type, may be about the same length as your typed manuscript. A book of poetry will be about the same length as your typed manuscript, if each poem is shorter than one page in length.

If you're writing a speech, one double-spaced page of typing will take you about two minutes to read out loud. It runs about 250 words. The script for a fifteen-minute speech should run no longer than seven and a half pages, double spaced, and you need to start wrapping it up when you hit the middle of page 6.

We encourage you to touch people's hearts in your own way, to find your own voice, and that's one reason we encourage you to break free from writing in a preconceived form. When a preconceived form becomes merely a formula, the way you express your feelings can become merely sentimental.

We dislike what we call sentimentality, but we struggle with it all the time, and we suspect that any writer who writes about moving experiences will struggle with it, too. We even have a hard time agreeing about what sentimentality is, exactly, although we think we know it when we see it.

We dislike sentimentality because we think it is an attempt to manipulate your reader artificially and predictably. We think it means something other than authenticity, and we encourage you to write authentically and truly from your heart in your own way, not in somebody else's conventional words.

Greeting cards are a handy example of sentimentality. People who write verses for greeting cards have the task of expressing an emotion— a sentiment—in such a way that millions of greeting-card buyers will find it acceptably close to the way they would express their own feelings, or anyway, close to what they believe they *ought* to feel on Mother's Day or another occasion. The writers force feelings (authentic or not) into a formula, like stuffing a sausage.

Hollywood has made an industry of manipulating viewers' emotions. Paper moons and cardboard seas, string sections off stage, artful makeup and Vaseline on the lens are the devices of what we have come to call cheap sentimentality. Some audiences cry at the emotion expressed in tearjerkers and seven-hanky romances. Other viewers cry tears of rage at being manipulated.

Many of us got our first taste of writing from the little stories in

Reader's Digest that tug at your heartstrings, display a puppyish sense of humor, and hammer home a life lesson at the end. Even if we never thought, "when I grow up, I want to write like that," those stories imprinted a pattern in our brains that pops up every time we set out to express what we see, think, and feel.

It's hard to write about what you feel. It's the truest part of yourself but also the most vulnerable part, the part you may have spent years learning how to hide. In writing about your feelings, you may start out being sentimental—mushy, corny, flowery, gushy, melodramatic, bittersweet, maudlin, whatever you want to call it. As you dig deeper in your writing, we believe you will work past sentimentality toward simply and purely expressing what you yourself see, think, and feel.

26

In a gallery, each framed and matted photograph is displayed behind a pane of clear glass. As you pause to study an Ansel Adams print, you see the moonrise, the clouds in a dark sky, the mountains, and the low adobe houses of a village in northern New Mexico, and the glass is perfectly invisible.

But suppose the glass has not been polished recently and your eye focuses on a flyspeck or a thumbprint on the glass. That unexpected interference brings you back to the surface of the glass itself, back to the ordinary world, away from Hernandez, New Mexico, to the painted drywall, carpet, ceiling tiles, and air conditioning vents of the gallery itself.

Just so, readers peer through the clear glass of the words you have written, through the page on which words have been printed with type and ink, into a fascinating world revealed by the language.

A reader passes through the page into what we might call the reading state. The reader's attention strolls in the moonlight toward the village of the poem. He loses himself in a dreamlike place beyond the surface of the page, trancelike and timeless.

For readers to stay in that reading state, the writing itself must be transparent. Whenever the writer brings attention back to the surface of the page, the spell is broken.

One trick "to remain invisible," Elmore Leonard says, and "not distract the reader from the story with obvious writing," is never to use "a verb other than 'said' to carry dialogue. The line of dialogue belongs to the character; the verb is the writer sticking his nose in."

Following conventions of grammar and spelling helps to keep your writing transparent. (As horror novelist Stephen King says, you can find all the grammar guidance you need in Strunk and White, *The*

Elements of Style, and the endpapers of John E. Warriner's *English Composition and Grammar*.)

Yet even readers who never missed a day when the teacher was diagramming sentences on the blackboard may have to slow down and puzzle out a grammatical construction that seems obstinately complicated or a paragraph-long sentence with no punctuation such as this one.

A spelling error and syntax that's unclear, correct or not, and even a typographical error, writing *flower* for *flour*, are impositions that spoil your readers' experience, reminding them that they're reading a book. After puzzling them out, the reader has to settle back, make the writing transparent once more, and try to regain the magical reading state.

27   The Unexpected Detail

If each of us at a dinner party were to offer a detail for an imaginary scene, we would each come up with something pretty predictable. If I told you that for a communal poem we were going to imagine a landfill at the edge of town, I would expect you to supply details like plastic bags, beer cans, an old washing machine, and a grapefruit rind. We could assemble a calendar picture of a landfill that way, with everything we could imagine tossed in. It would be—sort of—convincing. But what would bring the scene to life and convince our readers that we had actually seen it would be to add a completely unpredictable detail. What if one person thought to look up in the sky. There it is, a yellow ultralight aircraft buzzing along five hundred feet in the air.

Notice as you read how often these unexpected details are used to authenticate scenes. You'll discover, especially in fiction, how often a writer will drop in something just to make a scene seem real. For example, if the protagonist of a novel is talking with another person on a sidewalk in a park, the writer may put in a sentence like, "A man with a bad limp stumbled past, being jerked ahead by a large and ill-groomed poodle."

Those unexpected details bubble up to the surface when a writer works more and more deeply into a scene, and a writer keeps them because they're useful. Walter Van Tilburg Clark, in his novel *The Ox-Bow Incident*, has a character arrive riding a mule. The narrator recognizes it's a mule by the sound of its footfalls, a clip-clip-clip, not a horse's clop-clop, and can identify the rider—he's the stagecoach driver Bill Winder, the only man in the territory who would ride a mule. Clark doesn't let it go there but sinks further into the scene. His narrator reflects that "there's something about a mule a man can't get fond of . . . it's like he had no insides, no soul," and then contemplates the fastidious character of Bill Winder himself: "Winder didn't like mules, either, but that's why he rode them. It was against his religion to get on a horse; horses were for driving."

28   It's a Figure of Speech

HAMLET:

Do you see yonder cloud that's almost in shape of a camel?

POLONIUS:

By the Mass, and 'tis like a camel, indeed.

HAMLET:

Methinks it is like a weasel.

POLONIUS:

It is backed like a weasel.

HAMLET:

Or like a whale?

POLONIUS:

Very like a whale.

In our working lives, all the memos, contracts, business letters, specifications, and insurance policies we write have to be accurate and precise. Any other kind of language runs the danger of being misleading and, even worse, costing our employers or ourselves money.

If a bureaucrat paused to consider whether a cloud really resembled a whale, then the boss might mock him as Hamlet mocks Polonius in William Shakespeare's play.

If a real-estate developer imitated Samuel Taylor Coleridge, in his poem "Kubla Kahn," and "a stately pleasure dome decreed," with "caverns measureless to man" and "forests ancient as the hills," his contractor would surely walk away muttering and shaking his head.

When you are writing information at the most elementary level, specifying how a thing is to be done (use velvet, not percale; saw the board 36 inches long, not 37.5 inches), or exactly what happened ("I arrived at 8:15 p.m."), then the writing needs to be accurate and precise, and you are in the realm of the concrete, literal truth.

But if you are writing about why things happened, or how they seemed to you—if you are stepping up the ladder from information to knowledge to wisdom, from physical sensations to emotions to ideas—you are leaving the world of objects and facts and entering the realm of appearances, the world as interpreted by your mind. A flat, literal statement can never quite convey your thoughts, your vision of the pleasure dome to be, the meaning you attach to things, your feelings and conceptions. Then, comparing clouds with whales, or forests with hills, lends force to your writing.

A comparison of this sort is what teachers call a figure of speech or a metaphor. There are many kinds of metaphor—in school some of us had to memorize all of their names. Essentially, a metaphor is a way of describing one thing in terms of another. You use metaphor to compare or contrast something you imagine, or something right in front of you, with something somewhere else. Your reader cannot read your mind or see what is right in front of you, and the metaphor refers the reader to something else both of you may have seen or experienced or imagined.

Metaphors add an elemental strength to your writing. Metaphors have been a fundamental building block of language since people first furrowed their brows to describe their world. They called something an acorn squash because it was a squash that looked like an acorn, just as an acorn nut is something that screws onto a bolt and looks like an acorn. In modern times a construction company called its products Acorn Houses, suggesting long-lived, mighty oak trees, smooth surfaces, seamless design, and other positive characteristics we associate with acorns and oaks.

People put metaphorical names on the land. The Snake River twisted like a snake when it was named, and it still does. Travelers on the old Santa Fe Trail used a landmark in New Mexico that they called Wagon Mound because it looked like a prairie schooner, and everyone passing by on Interstate 25 today can see the resemblance.

Metaphor is risky. Your reader may not have experienced the other thing exactly the way you have. You may say a truck roars like a thunderstorm because you love the power and glory of a thunderstorm, while your reader may find it terrifying.

But what outweighs the risk is that a vivid metaphor is compelling, so that the reader cries out, "Yes! Forests as ancient as the hills!" Your reader might visualize the Arbuckles, the old, old stubs of mountains in southern Oklahoma, imagine trees as old as those dusty hills, and exult in sharing a vision with you, the writer, even if the hills you have in mind are the green, rolling hills of West Virginia.

Or when you write that a mist was like a gauze, a reader may remember the mist floating past the gauze curtains at the window of her grandmother's spare bedroom, where the reader took a soothing nap long ago.

Metaphors cement a bond of associations with your readers and help them remember your writing, too.

The great thing about metaphor is that it gives you a way to get elusive feelings down on the page or into someone else's ear. Roly Sally, a musician, wrote a song he called "Killing the Blues." He sang about "Swinging the world by the tail / Bouncing it over a white cloud," and anyone who has experienced the rambunctious blues, as contrasted with the too-depressed-to-get-out-of-bed blues, surely knows what he means.

Metaphor can be an especially powerful tool of persuasion, as when John F. Kennedy described his presidency as the New Frontier (evoking a real frontier of coonskin caps and long rifles), and Martin Luther King Jr. proclaimed that he had been to the mountaintop (evoking Moses's view of the Promised Land in the Old Testament).

Closing the door on the concrete, literal world of business and setting out to write, you may have to introduce metaphor quite consciously into your writing. You may have to look for passages where metaphor can be introduced and ask yourself how vivid and apt your metaphor is. When I say that this coffee is thick and black as oil at the wellhead, can I clearly visualize oil at the wellhead? Is the coffee really more or less like oil?

In prose, you don't want to lay it on too thick. One whizbang metaphor every three or four double-spaced pages seems to keep readers alert. (In a way, poetry is all metaphor.)

As you work consciously with metaphor, you may find more and more often that an apt metaphor opens a door out of a box, gives you a way to express something difficult, a tool to convert something physical and visible into language that is abstract and portable, the same tool an old-timer used when he called a river a snake.

Metaphors are forceful. Similes are, like, casual. In a *metaphor*, you compare one thing with another by stating that the two things are precisely identical: my heart *is* a rose that blooms for you.

In a *simile*, the other common figure of speech, you say only that one thing is similar to another, using *like* or *as*: my love *is like* a red, red rose.

A simile sounds casual and conversational, like everyday speech, but it lacks the authority of a metaphor. Metaphors always sound more forceful than similes, which makes your writing sound more confident and forceful.

Speaking of metaphors, maybe everything's related to everything else . . .

Ralph Waldo Emerson wrote his poems and compelling essays in a room designed for the purpose, a capacious square study on the second story of his house in Concord, Massachusetts.

North light poured through the tall windows into Emerson's study. One wall, floor to ceiling, was devoted to Emerson's world-embracing library. A round writing table sat in the center of a carpet, placed so that the writer's back was warmed by the fireplace. Each drawer in the table held a current writing project, and the top of the table would rotate, so that Emerson could bring his day's work before him without moving from his chair.

From this room, Emerson traveled the world in the books he read and on his lecture tours. He crossed the Atlantic to Europe. He rode the train to California, he saw the Grand Canyon. He drew his experience into this study and then looked beyond the room again, and from all that he knew, Emerson suggested that there might be a plane of common unity among all things and occurrences that he called the Oversoul, and that all things might touch each other along that plane.

A hundred years later, physicists said something similar in a theory with the metaphorical nickname "the Big Bang." They suggested that all things in the Universe have spread forward in time from one highly compressed speck of matter. This means, they said, that all things are related, made up of the same elements and energies and governed by the same laws.

The poet and the physicists were both expressing a kind of faith, which we human beings find deeply satisfying, in universal order.

The most effective writing seems to reach through the opaque surface of the world and offer a glimpse of that universal order beyond.

The power of a metaphor may come not only in proportion to the distance between its elements, but also from the writer's use of controls, so that the dazzling spark that arcs from one side of the comparison to the other is a clean flash, not dimmed by extraneous matter floating in between. A writer's goal is to light up the sky.

29 Before Us on the Table

You open a book you have never read before, and you begin to read. Each new story or poem begins with a kind of bare table, well lighted, with darkness all around. As you begin to read, every noun gives you something to envision, and one thing after another appears on your table. Maybe, in the book you are reading, a chicken appears first, then a washing machine, and then a half-melted candle in the neck of a jug.

Start with the chicken. Let's say you read, "She had eyes like a chicken." Shazam! A chicken pops into your mind, and whatever personal associations you have with chickens appear as well. Maybe you remember the fierce gaze of a red rooster that bit you on the leg when you were a child—and the placid stare of the warm white hens your grandmother kept, pillowlike creatures that cackled in contentment when you reached for an egg. All your personal experiences with chickens begin to cluster around the word "chicken." The table of the book you're reading is suddenly populated with chickens—mean, friendly, red, black, or speckled, some you read about in books, the one your dog chased into the street, a delectable one you ate at your Great-Aunt Mildred's, panfried with mashed potatoes and gravy, followed by rhubarb pie.

So, you read, she had eyes like a chicken "and a heart like a washing machine." In your mind a washing machine starts rocking and gurgling under a heavy load of your grandmother's winter bedding. It's the first day of spring. Suddenly, though, in your mind there's another. This second washer is broken, its motor burned out, a dead machine pushed back into a damp cellar corner. This second one smells like mildew and the first like Rinso Blue.

We've already got a lot of chickens and a couple of washing machines on the table, and then there's that candle in the jug to deal with. It may be lighted in one association and snuffed out in another. Maybe in one of them there is the sound of Ravi Shankar playing the sitar and the smell of patchouli oil. Maybe in another there is a cold, dark room with a wick just then pinched out and a burning spot between your thumb and index finger. Maybe there's the candle that accidentally lit the bedroom curtains on fire and burned down the house.

This process of assembling associations goes on, stirred by noun after noun, as you read along. The table fills up and things get perilously close to falling off into oblivion. Though each private association may get crowded out as they accumulate, a kind of after-image of everything named has a way of lingering. After a few pages, your many private associations with chickens, washing machines, and candles may still be on the table, along with everything else the writer has called up. By the end of the story or poem, that candle may have been pushed off toward the edge of your awareness as a reader, but in your mind there still remains a wisp of smoke from a tiny red ember at the tip of its wick.

Most writers wish to achieve some definite effect upon their readers, and a reader's collective associations have a lot to do with the effect. How can a writer attempt to control the effect?

One way is to try to limit the variety of associations any noun may call up. The less clutter, the better. For example, if you intend to have a pleasant effect, you want to avoid conjuring up associations that produce an unpleasant effect. You want to avoid summoning up the ghost of a rooster that bit your reader till he bawled.

You can steer or regulate the effect of your nouns with adjectives, the words that modify or help to define nouns.

You may have been taught that adjectives make for weak writing, and it's true that an overabundance of adjectives can sap the strength of your writing, but adjectives can be extremely useful in limiting the number of associations that arise in a reader's mind.

If someone writes, "She had eyes like a chicken, cold and unblinking and glassy," those three adjectives (cold, unblinking, glassy) immediately steer the reader's associations away from those placid old laying hens toward a more dangerous chicken, one that shows a little of the reptile in its distant ancestry.

By using adjectives, a writer can reduce the number of chickens on the reader's table from a dozen to maybe one or two.

If you write, "She had a heart like a broken washing machine," the single modifier "broken" immediately excludes that pleasant gurgling, sloshing machine on your grandmother's side porch.

Adjectives that specify number are especially useful. It is much easier for a reader to envision three chickens than just chickens. Once you determine the kind of association you want to inspire, you want it to be as clear and vivid as possible. "Chickens" is murky; there could be three or three hundred.

Every noun evokes a complex of associations in a reader's mind. Dropping in a noun implies you've thought about its possible associations. Using adjectives sparingly and with precision can help to exclude the associations you don't want and at the same time make the remaining things on the table work toward the effect you want to achieve.

This isn't a license to use strings of adjectives. Too many adjectives do make writing flabby. If you think about it—and you ought to think about every word in the pieces you write—there is probably one good adjective that will push aside most superfluous associations and pin the tail directly on the donkey.

30

Be Positive, Emphatic, Clear, and Active

Readers are hungry to learn what you know. They want you to open up a world that is rich with information, knowledge, and wisdom, and they expect it to be wrapped in a story that keeps them interested.

Everybody knows that it's best to convey what you know clearly. Writing clearly can mean many things. It can mean writing positively, for one thing, and with emphasis. As well, because stories are about people doing things, it means remembering to write actively.

For example, when you reach a conclusion, state it. Clearly. And positively. And with emphasis.

This practice of expressing yourself positively is a craft that you learn a step at a time. First, every time you find "no" or "not" or "never" in your writing, try to get rid of it by stating the same notion positively. For example, rather than writing, "He was not very often on time," say, "He usually came late." We have sought to apply this lesson, which we have drawn from Strunk and White, *The Elements of Style*, in our own book. We have combed our manuscript, seeking to eradicate all negative statements, and we have caught most of them.

Expressing yourself positively will have a remarkable effect on your life. You may believe that what you think determines what you write. The reverse is also true. It turns out that writing positively leads you into the habit of thinking positively, and thinking positively leads you to behaving positively in other areas of your life.

Writing positively is a matter of details.

For example, positive writers prefer *and* to *or*. *And* is affirmative. *Or* suggests vacillation. *And* suggests forward movement. *Or* suggests hesitation.

They also avoid opening a paragraph or a chapter with *although*. The idea is to be positive first, and express your reservations (if any) later (if at all).

Being positive also means being confident, stating your own knowledge or interpretation first and waiting until later to acknowledge the people who support or disagree with you. Stand on your own two feet.

Rather than:

Although Turner disagrees, I have learned that mice dance sideways.

Try writing:

Mice dance sideways. (Turner disagrees.)

Paying attention to emphasis helps you write clearly, confidently, and positively.

The emphasis in English prose falls at the beginning and end of a clause, sentence, paragraph, chapter, article, story, or poem, and the first chapter of every book. A winning first page will carry your reader through some awkward paragraphs later on.

Being clear means sticking to the point.

Before you begin, write a one-page abstract of what you think you are going to write, and write even that abstract in vigorous prose.

Being clear means avoiding ambiguity. The reader is counting on you to be forthright.

As you write, you know when you are being vague—you fall back on jargon, your sentence structure gets tangled. Then you know it's time to rewrite for clarity.

Clear writing usually communicates better than fancy writing, and it's certainly OK to be plain: Use hearty Anglo-Saxon words and avoid Latinisms. Avoid jargon. Especially if you write complex sentences poorly, it's OK to write simple sentences.

Positive, clear, emphatic writing is also exact: Cite specific dates when you know them, rather than using such phrases as "the midtwenties." Rather than "numerous," say how many. Write about real people, places, and things. A page sprinkled with the capital letters that signal proper nouns—Herbert Hoover, Waterloo—tells your reader that you know exactly what you are writing about. Often the exact facts, if presented well, will speak for themselves. Then, when you do offer interpretation, it will be emphatic by being rare.

The positive, clear, emphatic, exact writing that keeps people learning is always active rather than passive. Anything you write will most likely be about people doing things. Write with nouns (*people*) and verbs (*to do*). Choose active verbs, which assign responsibility, and eschew passive verbs, which writers use to avoid assigning responsibility.

Active: He did it.
Passive: It was done.

Active: You told me to turn left!
Passive: I was told to turn left.

Active: I goofed.
Passive: Mistakes were made.

Your readers will learn best from stories that are positive, clear, emphatic, plain, exact, and active, and your stories will express your own pride in your work. In those stories you will look good and stand tall. They will exhibit your joy in the work.

31   Transformative Experience

The process of writing is a transformative experience. You transform your thoughts—your information, knowledge, and wisdom—into words, and in the process you express the meaning that you have found in your experience.

You transform the story itself as you sink into it, writing in your journal, revising, redrafting, teasing out the one thing that the story is about.

Often, a transformative experience is also the thing that you are most eager to write about, a moment when you changed. Maybe it was a point of decision when you (or some fictional character) decided to go climb a mountain or never to go skiing again. Maybe it was a moment when your feelings or beliefs changed—the moment when you fell in love or came to believe that war is wrong.

Reading, too, is a transformative experience.

Reading can lead to action. After reading your editorial, a reader may leap up from her chair and go join a picket line protesting a subway fare increase.

But reading is often a more subtle transformative experience. "I never thought of that," one reader may think. Or "Until I read this story, I misjudged motorcycle riders and pit bulls, too."

Writing is probably most effective when it is a transformative experience for both you and your reader—when you both learn something new, see the world and your lives in a new way.

SECTION SEVEN

Revision and Getting Help

Writing is like shoveling snow—all the details you want to write about accumulate so rapidly that you can't get them all down. You're not sure that they will come to you tomorrow, and you're not yet confident that you will have plenty of other things to write about if your memory fails.

Revising, on the other hand, is like carding wool or like combing out long strands of hair—raking out the tangles, the cockleburs and dirt, and leaving the long strands clean and smooth and straight so that a comb can pass through the long, smooth hair unencumbered.

Before you send a poem, story, essay, or chapter out in public, you will want to make sure its shirt is tucked in.

It's a rare first draft that can be published or even read in public. Almost every piece of writing needs some rewriting, rethinking, and polishing before it is ready to take center stage.

The first step in spotting the flaws in what you have written is a simple one. Set it aside and let it cool off for a while, the longer the better. Take a look at it after twenty-four hours if you must, tinker with it a little, then set it aside again for as long as you can stand to. As if you had put it in a petri dish, the longer you leave a piece of writing by itself the more spores of trouble will surface. If you can bear to do it, leave it alone till it begins to look as if somebody else might have written it. (Stephen King sets the first draft of his books aside for six weeks before writing the second draft.) Then you can see it for what it is, a creation independent of you. Writing has to be equipped to thrive on its own in a largely indifferent world. You can't be there with it, like its parent, offering explanations, saying to an unappreciative reader, "Yes, but here's what I meant . . ."

Just what should you expect to see when you look at your writing after it has rested for a time? All sorts of things: peculiar syntax, tortured grammar, illogical thinking, misspellings, wordiness, silliness, preciousness. You may discover that the sweet sounds and rhythms you heard in your head when you wrote it now sound lumpy and awkward. (If you want to, you can ask for a little help here. Have a friend read your piece aloud to you, without studying it first, then listen carefully to the way in which he or she accents the words and places emphasis. A piece that sounded beautifully smooth to you when you heard it in your head may sound like a pretty rough road when you hear it read aloud.)

Even when you are very pleased with what you have written, you can make it even better or larger or more inspired or smarter, as the writer Susan Sontag observes. In revising, Sontag says, "You try to be clearer. Or deeper. Or more eccentric. You try to be true to a world. You want the book to be more spacious, more authoritative. You want to winch yourself up from yourself. You want to winch the book out of your balky mind."

And what's the big hurry, anyway? When you're baking cinnamon rolls, you don't take the bowl of raw dough to your friends and ask them if they like it. You wait till the rolls have been baked and have cooled and you've put on a little icing. The truth is, nobody's waiting for you to press your writing into their hands. Nobody's hungry for it. It's likely that not a living soul has big expectations for the success of it other than you. Of course, you want your writing to be wonderful—a work of pure genius, beautiful, heartbreaking, memorable—and that's just the kind of writing your audience would like to read. So let time show you some of the things you can improve before handing it to somebody and being embarrassed by a problem, or two or three problems, that you couldn't see in the giddiness of having just written something you like.

But keep on writing. Start a new piece while you're waiting for an earlier one to age. Most of us are tempted to get approval before moving on. We want our mothers to praise our mud pies before we make any more. But if you're going to get better at writing, you have to write a lot. You have to press on. We all learn writing by writing. Isak Dinesen said, "Write a little every day, without hope, without despair."

Several years ago, a man was telling Ted about his uncle, a horseshoe-pitching champion. One day he asked the uncle how he'd gotten good at horseshoes, and his uncle said, "Son, you got to pitch a hundred shoes a day." That's what it takes to get good at writing, too. You've got to pitch your hundred shoes a day.

Get with the process: Put your new poem, story, or essay in a file folder of its own and start work on the next one. When you finish a draft, or get stuck, put it in its own folder. After a month or so, you'll have a stack of folders on the side of your desk and can start looking through them, beginning with the oldest. You'll be amazed at the way the passage of time has helped you come up with solutions to problems you had during the writing of those early drafts.

33 Getting Advice, Taking Criticism

You write, you read what you have written, then you rewrite again and again. It's just you, alone with your story or essay or poem, hour after hour. Eventually you think you've done everything in your power to make what you've written as good as it gets.

When Stephen King was in high school, the editor of the Lisbon, Maine, *Weekly Enterprise* offered him this advice: write with the door closed, rewrite with the door open. That is, you write the first draft for yourself, and you revise to communicate with others.

Writing with the door open, you'll want to show what you have written to somebody. Writing is, after all, communication, and it's natural to want to know how well you've communicated. So go ahead, ask.

Writing can be like folding a banquet-sized tablecloth; you can do it yourself, but it's a lot easier when you can find somebody to help. Both beginning and veteran writers need help, and the acknowledgments page of any book will show you how grateful they are for receiving it.

University professors show their writing to their peers to get technical advice, but you are seeking something other than peer review, and it may be best if the first person you ask to read your work isn't a writer and doesn't have an English professor's vocabulary of critical terms. The slightest hint of disapproval from a "professional" can stop you in your tracks just when you need to be writing away, brave and free, and improving every day.

Your first reader does have to be somebody you can trust to be honest. And the reader should expect to put time and energy into reading your work and talking with you about it. You might ask your spouse, a neighbor, a good-humored friend, or another beginning writer to look at your efforts. Stephen King says that he asks his wife and five other friends to read and comment on a draft of every book he writes.

Your writing needs, first, to be understandable and interesting. Above all, you want your first reader simply to tell you where your writing makes sense and holds his or her attention—where it reaches across the ever-present gulf between a writer and a reader.

It's tempting to ask, "Is this any *good*?" But the last thing you need is a value judgment, and anyway, what reader will answer that one candidly? (Even when you submit your work to an editor, you're still not seeking a value judgment. The question is not whether the editor thinks it's any good but whether the editor believes it will benefit his or her readers.)

Instead of asking your first reader to rate your piece on some kind of scale from one (awful) to ten (terrific), you need to ask questions like "Is this clear?" and "How can I make this more interesting?"

You need a first reader who will take the time to answer those questions candidly, and with specifics. "Well, it's really diff'rent!" is just too vague. You want somebody who will say, "In the third paragraph of page 2, well, this may seem like a dumb question, but what do you mean by the word 'salutary?'" You need to encourage your reader to ask dumb questions—and to thank him when he does.

Specific comments are far more useful than general ones. When somebody does tell you "I really like this!" you might as well enjoy the comment. And then ask the tough questions. "What was it exactly that you liked? Was there anything you didn't like, maybe just a little?"

Librarians in the state of Kentucky once decided to produce a series of books to use in teaching adults how to read. They engaged professional writers, and then they showed the manuscripts, not to educational experts but to adults who were just learning how to read. They sat the writers and the student readers down face to face and had the writers listen to what the students had to say. The writers sweated bullets, we've heard, because they had never confronted their readers quite so directly, and the students, all adults who wanted desperately to learn, did not hesitate to say very directly what they needed from the books. The new readers wanted stories about a world they could relate to, and they wanted them to be clear and full of concrete detail. You want a first reader with the commitment of those beginning readers in Kentucky.

If you and your reader are both beginning writers, you will have to teach one another to appreciate the value of specific comments. Though it's nice to receive praise, what you both really need is, "I don't understand how the umbrella stand got over under the parlor window when a couple of paragraphs back it was just inside the kitchen door." Specific comments like that are invaluable. Another valuable criticism might be, "It takes you two paragraphs to describe how Doctor Abraham pushed his chair up to the table. Do you really want to spend that much time moving a chair? Unless that chair is a lot more important than I think it is . . ."

Your reader may offer comments that are more specific if she can read your piece at her own convenience and write notes for you to study later. Reading and criticizing somebody's writing requires concentration, and anyway, nobody appreciates being put on the spot. Shoving a manuscript under someone's nose and immediately demanding to know what she thinks is simply not good form. You two may find you get the most out of your writing friendship by writing letters to each other instead of meeting face to face. In a letter, you can study and restudy your reader's comments.

When you see that the reader is being candid, and when the reader sees that you are willing to take her comments and revise, you will both gain confidence in your working relationship. Then you can ask more pointed questions—"Are there places where your mind drifted away?" and "What would you omit?" and "What more would you like to know?" And the reader's comments can be more telegraphic—a simple "I dunno" or "wow," a check mark on the page, or a "more or less" wobble of the hand will tell you what you need to know.

One productive way to obtain criticism and encouragement is to join or start a writing group. If you ask around among your friends and acquaintances—and their friends—you are sure to find others who like to write, are eager for encouragement, and want to get better at it. Churches, public libraries, YWCAS, community college courses, professional associations, and informal groups (the mothers of your children's friends?) are good places to start.

When you have identified four or five people who are writing, you can suggest getting together once a month to talk about your efforts.

And four or five people are all you need.

If you take turns having a piece of writing ready to discuss at each meeting, all the members of the group are likely to come prepared to offer considered opinions, and each meeting will be briefer than if you try to discuss a piece by each member at each meeting. But if your group has more than a half dozen members, any member may grow weary of having to wait seven or eight weeks before presenting a new piece.

You might consider setting up a writers' group by e-mail, but the rules of engagement, and especially of decorum, need to be very clear. E-mail lends itself quite readily to ill-considered, hurtful, and even inflammatory comments that don't help anybody.

Different people come to a writers' group with different purposes. One writers' group, which has been meeting regularly for five years, came together through the professional connections of one of the members. It has five members:

> a young man for whom writing is one of several artistic avocations, along with sculpture and photography, and who publishes some of what he writes

> a woman who loves beautiful things and who expresses her thoughts and feelings in poems with little intention of publishing them

> a woman who, with the group's encouragement, has written a book about her own intense experiences that she is determined to publish

> a man who knows that he is a good writer with many stories to tell and who is looking for the next step to take with his writing

> a man who, in retirement, is undertaking writing as a second profession, but with little expectation of income from writing

One member of the group still remembers how thrilled she was to come to the first meeting to talk about her work with other writers.

Like any group of human beings, this writers' group began with a period of adjustment while the members got comfortable with one another and with the group.

Every six weeks or so, the group meets in the home of a different member for dinner and constructive criticism.

Each member of the group sends (usually by e-mail) a new piece of writing to all the other members well before a scheduled meeting. At the meeting, the group discusses each piece and often gives the writer notes on a copy of the piece.

The members of the group all encourage each other and give each other very careful and thoughtful practical criticism, usually about clarity and about highlighting the most engaging parts of the piece of writing. They also make very specific suggestions about rewriting the piece.

Members of the group agree that the feedback feels objective, never malicious, cruel, or hurtful, and that in receiving it the members have learned not to be defensive and simply to listen to one another.

Perhaps because the members of the group have built a strong bond of friendship and because they come to the group with such different purposes, they do not compete with each other as writers. Instead, they compete as hosts, seeing who can present the most delectable dinner. One can be counted on for Vietnamese food, another for Indian cuisine, and another for healthy fare, always featuring a fresh green salad.

This group has learned three essential rules of a successful writers' group:

1. Encourage each other.

2. Make specific constructive criticism—not "I really like this" or "I don't much care for that" but "Your first paragraph seems like you're just warming up to write the next paragraph. Perhaps you should consider starting with the second paragraph."

3. Have fun.

Another group of nearly twenty playwrights has been operating for thirteen years under very different rules. Their goal is performance of the plays they write. Their meetings are so earnest and focused that some newcomers find them intimidating, and they observe strict rules. They criticize only complete plays, not works in progress. They direct all comments to a designated facilitator, not to the writer. They do not rewrite each other's work. A writer seeking particular help must list his or her questions in writing. They don't share dinner, but after their meetings they often retire to a coffeehouse.

When you show up for your first writers' group meeting, take a deep breath before you ring the doorbell and prepare for constructive criticism and not for praise. Of course you want praise. The desire for praise and adulation, even love, is one of a writer's chief drives. And if it comes, enjoy it. But if somebody says, "I think this story is really wonderful," it's fair play to ask, "Could you tell me what about it you find wonderful?" When somebody says you've done something well, you need to know just what that something is, specifically, so you can do it again.

The words "good" and "bad" don't help much. When people say, "I just read a really good story" or "That's a bad poem," what they are really saying is that, perhaps for personal reasons, they like it or they don't. Perhaps they like the manner in which it is written. Perhaps they don't like the effect it has on them. We have individual likes and dislikes about practically everything. Some people dislike broccoli because they don't like the way it feels in the mouth. But does that make broccoli bad?

In addition to friends, relatives, and writing groups, you can sometimes engage a perfect stranger as a reader. If you can team up with another writer to exchange work, you can "pay for" the help you receive by helping the other person.

Many writers have maintained lifelong associations with other writers to their mutual benefit. Ted opened a correspondence with another poet, named Leonard, by sending him a note complimenting a poem he'd seen in a magazine. Since then, Ted and Leonard, living in Nebraska and California, have been exchanging their work for more than thirty years, and both of them have found the correspondence extremely helpful. Leonard gives Ted specific comments, not general praise or disapproval. For example, Leonard has suggested that Ted make the title of a poem carry some of the expository or narrative weight of a poem—rather than "A Winter Night," which tells little about the subject of the poem, perhaps call it "A Snowy Night in Milwaukee." Ted rarely submits a poem for publication that Leonard hasn't seen and criticized.

SECTION EIGHT

The Business of Writing

34   How Publishing Works

Why are you writing? More than likely, you want to tell someone how you feel. Maybe you have a moving story to tell. Maybe you want to pass along information, knowledge, or wisdom that will change your reader's life. Either way, you want to touch someone else's heart.

Touching someone else's heart is why young men write poems to girls and grandmas set down their memories for their granddaughters to read. Those written poems and memoirs are just a step away from what a young man would say in person, reciting a poem on bended knee, or a grandma would talk about while snuggling in a rocking chair. The young man and the grandma, speaking straight from their hearts to the heart of one person they love, have no need to be published.

Writers who want to touch the hearts of a lot of people, though, usually need many copies of what they have written. They need to be published.

Publishing means making broadly available, and it lets people read what you have written any time, anywhere, in privacy. (In the past, publishing always meant making multiple copies. Nowadays it can mean posting a message on the Web, where many people can find it.)

You may want to publish your writing because you have something new to say, have an original way to say it, hope to make an income, or just want your voice to be heard. But most likely you want your writing to be published because it's the end of the writing process. Fish gotta swim, birds gotta fly, athletes gotta compete, singers and actors gotta perform, writers gotta get published.

At the thought of publishing, many new writers turn pale with anxiety. Does that sound like you? If so, we'll bet there are two big reasons for your anxiety.

First, we've talked in many different ways about developing the habit of writing. We'll bet you're anxious because you're not yet in the habit of submitting your writing for publication. It hasn't yet become a routine part of your writing process. The more experience you have with the process, the less anxious you will become.

Second, we'll bet that you have a very lofty goal in mind—a certain idea of the publisher, or the magazine, where you want to be published—and in your imagination you've already spent the income on a sailboat or a new kitchen.

You're like a rookie baseball player, stepping up to the plate to bat against a really good pitcher—Randy Johnson, perhaps, the Big Unit. It's an opportunity to be a hero—or to humiliate yourself—in full view of thirty thousand fans in the stadium and millions more watching on TV. Sheer terror. You've never faced a fastball like his, and your job is to swing for the fences, to hit a home run. Right?

Wrong, probably, on both counts. First, by the time you face Randy Johnson, you will have spent hours and hours of your life in batting practice, working on the fundamentals, swinging at all kinds of pitches. So you will have seen plenty of fastballs a whole lot like his. And second, your job is not to belt a home run, but just to get on base.

Bil Gilbert, a friend we've mentioned before, is a prizewinning writer, and he also once coached his daughters' softball teams. Bil says that whenever he overheard the opposing coach say to a batter, "OK, in this situation we really need a home run," he knew he had 'em beat. Because Bil coached the fundamentals. "Keep your chin down," he urged his batters. "Keep your eye on the ball. Swing through the ball."

We're going to follow Bil's example. We're not going to say, "OK, now it's time to make your coaches look like heroes and hit a home run," and we're certainly not going to get up in your face and shout "Don't choke!"

Instead, we're going to say this: publishing is part of the writing process. You learned to write every day. You learned to write as if you were telling a story to a stranger. You learned to show your writing to others, to ask for and to listen to criticism. You learned to see writing as a way of making friends.

You're already practicing the fundamentals: how do you get published? By making friends. To plug what you have written into the network of published writing—to make friends with your readers—

you need first to plug into a network yourself by making friends with an editor. To make friends, it helps to understand a little about the editor's work.

The editor of your church newsletter and the fiction editor of a New York publishing house both have the same job—to select what they will publish. In making their choices, they weigh many factors—content, writing style, length of the manuscript, timing, fame and aptness of the writer, possible market, cost budgets, profit targets, and what readers might expect to see in the editor's magazine or book list.

You'll improve your chances of publication markedly by being sure that you are submitting your work to an appropriate publisher. When an editor rejects a manuscript, it's usually because the writer has simply submitted it to the wrong publisher: a poem submitted to a magazine that doesn't publish poetry, a knitting article sent to a cooking magazine, a six-thousand-word article offered to a magazine with an upper limit of fifteen hundred words per article.

When an editor asks for revisions, it means that the article or book meets many of the editor's criteria. It's not a rejection. It's not an unreserved acceptance, but it is an expression of interest.

The editor who has accepted your manuscript (sometimes called the acquiring or sponsoring editor) passes your manuscript along to another kind of editor, the copyeditor (who may be called a manuscript editor or line editor).

The copyeditor marks up your manuscript, checking for a multiplicity of things—spelling, grammar, consistency, felicity of expression, accuracy, plausibility, logic—and may ask the author to reconsider, reorganize, double-check, or delete some statements, paragraphs, or chapters.

Probably the sponsoring editor will have required you to submit the manuscript electronically, and the copyeditor will spend some time cleaning up your electronic files and marking them up to indicate how text, headings, quotations, and paragraphs ought to be treated typographically.

Before the days of computers, a physical manuscript was passed hand to hand from sponsoring editor to copyeditor to designer to typesetter to proofreader, and those several pairs of eyes were all alert to correcting errors. With computers, those jobs have merged. One editor may do all of those jobs, and nobody in the publishing house may actually read your article or book word for word, so it's up to you to make sure that your work is true and beautiful.

When an editor does devote time, energy, and skill to helping you write better, you should count yourself lucky—and be sure to say thanks.

The writer doesn't usually get involved in the printing and distribution of magazines and books, which involve relationships that the publisher has developed over many years with specialized printers (full-color long-run magazine printers, for instance), wholesalers, and bookstores, but the author can have a distinct role to play in the marketing of books.

A book publisher's marketing system—catalogs, ads, sales representatives, publicity—is built on routine. It is geared to getting the word about hundreds of books out to millions of people. It is not built for customized campaigns to sell a niche book or to reach a niche market.

You, the writer, can play a tremendously useful role in helping to make the marketing routine work for your book.

You can write a book that has a large, identifiable readership, and you can give the publisher an apt picture of the market you intend the book to reach.

You can establish your own identity among the readers you intend to reach—writing articles and op-ed pieces and giving speeches related to your book, even dressing in costume—a white linen suit and a panama hat if your name is Tom Wolfe.

You can provide accurate lists of magazines that might review the book; groups, from readers' groups to professional organizations, that might be a market; and names and addresses of relatives, friends, and colleagues who might buy the book.

You can appear in public and autograph books, not just in bookstores but at places and events related to your topic.

And you can listen to your publisher's advice, especially about having realistic expectations for the sale of your book.

One writer of children's books has spent years trekking to elementary schools reading her work, autographing books in shopping malls and theaters, making her books well known, and turning her identity as an author into a brand name that grandparents, parents, and children all recognize. She has done all of this work with a big smile on her face, sometimes in costume. She even devised a clever couple of words to write in a book she is autographing. No sales rep could have done what she has done to make her books a success.

Despite all the skill and commitment that you and the publisher devote to publishing, any issue of a magazine is ephemeral and the market for almost every book is finite. That's OK, too, because, working on the fundamentals, you learned that your job is not to hit a home run. Your job is to get on base. Right?

You will probably not make any money as a writer. Most writers receive nothing more than free copies of the magazine that published their poems and stories. A smaller number of writers receive modest fees, between fifty and several hundred dollars, for their work. An even smaller number of writers of books sign contracts in which the publisher promises to pay royalties for every copy sold.

Only a very few writers realize enough money from writing to make much difference in the way they live.

Say a magazine pays $500 per story. Say you sell that magazine four stories per year. That's $2,000, less taxes (say, 20 percent), for a net of $1,600 per year, or $133.33 per month. To get a notion of how this income would affect your life, you might look up your most recent monthly credit card bill. What percentage of the bill does $133.33 represent?

You'd receive the same amount of income, $2,000 before taxes, if a book publisher paid you a royalty of 10 percent of retail price, the book retailed for $20, and the publisher sold 1,000 copies.

For income tax purposes you ought to keep fairly accurate records of the expenses and income associated with your writing. Your accountant can advise you about the tax implications of your life as a writer.

Anyway, you want to publish your writing, not for the money, but to touch someone's heart. So how do you get published?

You have completed a manuscript that you believe strangers will want to read. You've completed a process of thinking, writing, taking the advice of your readers, revising. Congratulations! Next comes publishing what you have written. Getting published is a process, too, with its own steps for the writer to take.

The Writer's Role in Getting a Manuscript Published

Placing your work with a publisher is like marketing. Marketing experts know that billboards alone don't sell a product. Neither do space ads in newspapers and magazines. Neither do junk mail, bus cards, or phone solicitation. Neither, solely, does public relations, although the goal of PR—the buzz, the grapevine, positive word of mouth—is the most powerful marketing tool in the world.

What ultimately sells any product, including your book, is a combination of several media. That means making yourself and your writing known by exploiting a combination of avenues:

Publish your writing everywhere you can—in newsletters, local newspapers, specialized magazines. Whether or not you get paid for your writing, you are accumulating experience, and you can list all those publications in your résumé. And you are building a readership—what in the music business they call a fan base.

Most writers will have published lots of small pieces—articles, poems, short stories—before they publish their first book. To pick just one example, Emily Carter's publisher, Coffee House Press, touted her first book as her debut. But she had already published short stories in the *New Yorker*, *Story Magazine*, *Gathering of the Tribe*, and other magazines, and Garrison Keillor had selected the title story, *Glory Goes and Gets Some*, for *The Best American Short Stories 1998*. Emily Carter had lived a lifetime as a writer before she even got a debut.

A poet will publish every single poem in magazines before putting together a book manuscript, and the author of a nonfiction book may well have published at least one-third of the material as articles.

Become known as an expert. Talk about the subject of your work at every opportunity—at your church, at Rotary meetings, at seminars. Become known. Think of your name as a brand—Stephen King, Barbara Cartland, Dave Barry, Barbara Kingsolver—and think how you want your brand to be identified.

Stephen King sells horror mysteries.

Barbara Cartland sells bodice rippers.

Dave Barry sells guy humor.

Barbara Kingsolver sells stories about women and the environment.

Then think what attributes you want to promote in your work.

Maybe you write children's novels that transform school-day anxieties by placing them in the magical world of a wizard named Harry Potter.

Maybe you write clever cowgirl adaptations of fairy tales with a feminist spirit.

Maybe you write lighthearted travel books about Latin America from a left-wing point of view.

Articulate the *single unique feature* of your book or article. Beginning writers, especially, reflect on all the ideas, feelings, and observations they put into their work, and they have to try over and over to find its single unique feature.

Introduce yourself to editors and agents by letter, or in person at writers' workshops, when you are deciding where to submit a manuscript for publication.

Whether you plan to publish where you can submit your writing directly to the editor (with many magazines and most university presses, for example), or where the editors prefer to work with agents (in most commercial book publishing houses, for example), it's a good idea to become known among both editors and agents.

The more clearly and sympathetically you have established your brand, the more readily you will find an agent, the more profitably an agent can work for you, and the easier it will be to achieve publication, with or without an agent.

Many beginning writers hope that if they can only attract an agent their troubles will be over. An agent's access to editors, knowledge of publishing, and experience negotiating contracts—those are all indeed valuable.

But the agent is only one of many resources the writer taps to achieve success, and having an agent may not even be essential to success. One successful writer we know has long had an agent, but even so he schedules regular trips to New York to make the rounds of editors himself. Stephen King says that he didn't have an agent until he had already earned three million dollars from his writing.

What agents cannot do is the one thing beginning writers would like them to do. An agent cannot take away the pain of rejection. Instead of rejection by an editor, a writer faces the prospect of rejection by agents—and editors' rejections passed along by an agent. One friend's agent, after repeated tries, failed to place his novel and sent him a dozen editors' rejections in a single manila envelope. As one rejection letter after another spilled out into his lap, the writer laughed about it, but it was a wry laugh at best.

Even so, the first question at any writers' conference is usually, How do I get an agent? There are four ways writers connect with an agent:

1. The agent comes to you. Agents read widely, looking for writers to represent, and an article you publish in a magazine (even an online magazine) may strike a chord with an agent, who may write asking to represent you.

2. You scan the list of agents in such reference books as *Literary Market Place* and *Writers' Market*, available at the reference desk of most public libraries, looking for agents who list specialties similar to yours.

3. You read the acknowledgments in books by your favorite current writers. An agent who represents one or two of those writers may be the agent you would like to have representing you, too.

4. You attend writers' conferences and workshops, planning to meet agents and to present them with book proposals.

With any of these four approaches, you take matters into your own hands, choosing a reputable agent who will represent you well.

Any of these approaches will involve some networking—taking the advice of friends who have agents, attending workshops, corresponding with many agents, making appointments, traveling to New York—and lots of reading.

Having identified an agent, or a list of agents, you'd like to have representing you, it's up to you to sell or pitch your work to the agent.

You can pitch your work to an agent just as you would to an editor. The most important element is a good presentation—a letter that you write and rewrite to get just the right tone. If you have done your job right, an agent will respond to your queries or will come to you.

Of course, there is no guarantee that every writer will attract an agent. To stay in business, first-class literary agents must choose clients who will earn, and consequently will earn the agent, a substantial income over a period of many years.

Agents look especially for writers at the beginning of their careers—the next young Stephen King or Joyce Carol Oates—who, over the course of a lifetime, may write dozens of best sellers. A writer starting out at age sixty-one has fewer years to write than does one starting out at twenty-five—an obstacle your pitch may need to overcome, perhaps by an emphasis on the experience of the world that you bring to your writing.

Whether you are seeking an agent or an editor, what you are doing is finding a match—a process that takes time.

For writers submitting work directly to magazines, it means sending out lots of stories, poems, and queries, and being prepared for rejection.

We know one beginning writer who didn't merely brace himself for rejection, he planned for it. He set out, during his first year as a writer, to send out one submission per week, and he planned to receive fifty-two rejections during the year. He failed to meet his goal. He had only forty-eight rejections—because he also received four thrilling, major, national acceptances.

One way to begin is to seek out every possible opportunity to publish your work. To build experience and a track record, you can submit poems to small magazines, opinion pieces to the local newspaper, book reviews to the church newsletter. One woman in Tucson wrote half a dozen columns about her Mexican American family's place in the community and submitted them to the editor of the afternoon daily newspaper. He hired her to write a weekly column about Mexican American life in Tucson.

At the same time, you can submit your work to national magazines, whether they are specialized journals, little poetry magazines, or general interest magazines such as *Harper's*, *Atlantic Monthly*, and the *New Yorker*.

To protect their time, most editors ask that writers send a query seeking permission to submit an article or story before actually sending the piece itself. (Nowadays, editors generally prefer to receive queries, and manuscripts, too, by e-mail, although a few still prefer queries and manuscripts on paper.) An editor can tell quickly from a brief query whether the subject of a writer's proposal is in the ballpark. More often than not, when an editor rejects a piece of writing it's because the subject doesn't fit the interests of the magazine or publisher—the writer has simply sent the piece to the wrong publisher.

A great many magazines post their writers' guidelines on a Web site, and writers can e-mail a query and receive a prompt response.

It's common sense and common courtesy to submit a piece to only one magazine at a time. As a reader, you probably know the one magazine where you would most expect to see your article or story. Likewise, it's best to send a query (as distinct from a complete piece of writing) to only one magazine at a time.

Poets often have half a dozen packets of poems, five or ten poems per packet, simultaneously circulating to magazines, each packet submitted to only one magazine at a time.

In your one-page query letter, which you can customize to go to several editors simultaneously, you should do six things:

1. Ask the editor if you may please submit your article or story for the editor to consider for publication, always giving the title of the piece and its length in words.

2. Describe the submission in one or two sentences, focusing on the single unique feature of the piece—what it's got that no other story has.

3. Say why you are submitting the piece to that particular magazine.

4. Identify yourself as a writer. (Toot your own horn without apology. You're a brand name, remember?)

5. Ask to hear from the editor.

6. Say "thank you."

Writing a query letter is just like writing a poem, an article, or a story. It's hard work, and it deserves every ounce of your ability and attention. You should spend ample time crafting your query letter.

The query letter for a nonfiction piece should state succinctly, in addition to the single unique feature of your manuscript, your single greatest qualification for writing it (including a list of some of the places where you have previously published). It may be only when you compress your work into a query letter that you realize what you're really trying to say and why you're qualified to say it. It's like a plug on the six o'clock news. You have just a few seconds to tell your story in a compelling way. Like this:

Dear [editor's name goes here]:

May I please submit my article "Jane Doe and Her Friends in Sonora" (2,500 words) for publication in [magazine title]?

My article tells the unique story of an American woman who, through microcredit—making tiny loans to a circle of women in a squatter settlement on our border with Mexico—helps them learn to improve their lives, from hygiene to hairdressing.

U.S. Sen. Hillary Rodham Clinton is among the Americans who, like Jane Doe, have embraced microcredit as a means of lifting the poorest of the poor from poverty. Your readers may appreciate learning about this interest of Senator Clinton's.

Ms. Doe works in Mexico as a volunteer. Her professional work is equally affecting—she practices physical therapy with the elderly and with victims of torture and leprosy.

I have recently published more than twenty general interest articles on master teachers such as Ms. Doe and the U.S. border with Mexico.

May I hear from you soon? A stamped, self-addressed envelope is enclosed.

Thank you for considering my proposal for [magazine title].

Sincerely yours,
[your signature]

An e-mail query, like every e-mail message, needs to be especially succinct, no more than one screen long. And of course, be sure to give your address and phone number in your e-mail.

After the editor has replied to your query by inviting the article, nowadays you may well submit the article by e-mail. Otherwise, you put the article in an envelope with a one-page cover letter and a self-addressed, stamped envelope. You address the envelope to the editor, affix sufficient postage to both envelopes, and put the packet in the mail.

Your one-page cover letter (or the opening of your submission e-mail) should do the same six things as a query letter. Like this:

> Dear [editor's name goes here]:
>
> Thank you very much for offering to consider the enclosed article, "Jane Doe and Her Friends in Sonora" (2,500 words), for publication in [magazine title].
>
> [Repeat the body of your query letter.]
>
> Again, thank you very much for considering my work. May I hear from you soon? A stamped, self-addressed envelope is enclosed.
>
> Sincerely yours,
> [your signature]

Submitting a manuscript to a book publisher is similar. The first step is a book proposal, a more elaborate version of a magazine query letter. The agent Michael Larsen's book, *How to Write a Book Proposal*, is an excellent comprehensive guide. It's in our list of Further Reading at the back of the book. A book proposal can be quite elaborate; at its simplest, it can comprise

> A one-page cover letter focusing on the single unique, compelling feature of your book, your qualifications for writing it, and the core readership that you are addressing
>
> An outline presented as a series of narratives—a paragraph of one or two sentences about each chapter. A narrative outline will give the editor an idea of your skill as a writer and the flow of the book.

Two or three sample chapters—the most compelling actual chapters of the book, not photocopies of previously published articles that you plan to recycle as chapters of the book but haven't yet rewritten. One of them can be, but need not be, the introduction.

A one-page résumé emphasizing your experience as a writer and your qualifications to write this particular book

A stamped, self-addressed envelope

You can send a book proposal to several publishers at one time. But out of consideration for the time and energy an editor will put into considering it, you should submit a full book manuscript to only one publisher at a time.

Much of this correspondence—the query letter, the outline and sample chapters, even the completed manuscript—can be conducted nowadays by e-mail.

While you are waiting for replies you have an opportunity to keep writing. As a writer you will have many irons in the fire, more than one string to your bow, lots of stories, novels, articles, and books in the works or going out to publishers, either getting published or rejected and being readied to be sent out again somewhere else.

How to Choose a Publisher

In choosing a publisher, the best place to start is with the magazines you like to read and the publishers that have published the books you love.

If you are writing nonfiction, matching the topical interests of the magazine or publisher is especially important. Most of the queries editors reject are for material that simply doesn't fit their focus in terms of subject matter. Health magazines tend to publish articles about health, crafts magazines about crafts, retirement magazines about topics of presumed interest to retired persons.

Fiction and poetry are more matters of taste than of topic, but reading through one or two recent issues of a magazine will give you a notion of whether your work is likely to be welcomed by its editors.

Second to the topical focus of the publisher is the length of manuscripts they publish.

General interest magazines nowadays want articles of 1,500 words (6 double-spaced pages) or less.

A book for adults is more than 33,250 words (133 double-spaced pages) long.

If your manuscript stands between 6 and 132 pages, before you go any further you may want to shorten it to fit a magazine or fatten it to make a book.

There are many exceptions. The manuscript of a children's book can be much shorter than 133 pages, and so can the manuscript for a book of poems. A few specialized journals publish articles longer than 6 pages. If you are already extremely famous, editors are likely to stretch their criteria.

A writer's first step on the road to becoming extremely famous is publishing in magazines.

How to Choose a Magazine

The *New Yorker* sprang to mind, right? If you want to hit the big time, you think first of the mass circulation, general interest magazines—*Harper's*, the *Atlantic Monthly*, the *New Yorker*—because they publish writing that interests you and a million people like you. Also, you may have heard that they pay well. Nothing wrong with that—go ahead and give it a shot.

But these three magazines publish only an exquisitely small amount of the writing produced every month, and staff writers or regular contributors write a lot of what they do publish, and every writer in the world is sending them stuff, so the odds are very long against your scoring the first time out.

You can think of those three as the pinnacle of a pyramid of magazines.

The second-tier magazines are slightly more specialized. They're addressed primarily to either women (*Cosmopolitan*, *Ladies' Home Journal*, *Redbook*) or men (*Esquire*, *Playboy*, GQ).

A third tier comprises still more specialized magazines, such as *Parents*, *Working Mother*, and *Horse & Rider*, that pay their writers and might be slightly more hospitable to new writers than the top three. Typically, their Web sites will offer writers' guidelines.

And so the pyramid goes, each tier built of ever more numerous and more specialized magazines. (Blogs and other kinds of publishing on the Internet can fit many places on the pyramid, from general interest writing for a large audience to specialized writing for a tiny readership.)

The foundation of the pyramid is a mass of thousands of extremely specialized magazines, each with a circulation of one thousand or fewer. The few subscribers to any one magazine, and the few advertisers wishing to reach them, provide the publishers with very little money, and these magazines in turn may pay their writers next to nothing.

These small-circulation magazines are fertile ground for a novice writer who simply wishes to communicate or who wants to develop her skills while on the road to greater glory and income as a writer. Laura Hillenbrand, the author of the best seller *Sea Biscuit*, which became a successful movie, established her reputation by writing non-fiction articles for specialized horse magazines. Also, if your specialized writing is a good match for a specialty magazine, you can publish a lot with relatively few rejection slips.

To choose magazines to submit to, first inventory the magazines you receive and note two or three where your writing would fit. Study the fine print in an issue of each magazine to find the name of the editor, address of the editorial offices (as distinguished from the office of advertising, circulation, or publisher), and Web address. You may also find brief guidelines for writers.

Second, scan the racks of a newsstand and the shelves of current periodicals in your public library and get editors' names and addresses from a few relevant magazines.

While you're at the public library, you can find the shelf of *Writer's Market* and similar reference books. These books offer magazine editors' advice about what writing they want to see and how to submit, along with other information. These books are not comprehensive—they focus on outlets that pay writers—so you may find only a few magazines related to your interests.

Third, an Internet search, using Google and other search engines, may uncover additional magazines in your area of interest, and you may also find Internet sites where you can publish your writing.

At this point, you have selected a half dozen magazines where you'd like to publish your writing.

If you haven't been able to find the name and address of a magazine's editor, or guidelines for writers, you might check the magazine's Web site.

As only one example, we found *Reminisce: The Magazine that Brings Back the Good Times* with an Internet search (the Web site is www.reminisce.com). We'd never heard of the magazine, but plenty of people have—it claims more than a million subscribers. We also found the very comprehensive writers' guidelines for *Reminisce* at their Web site.

In positive, exact, and plain language, the *Reminisce* contributors' guidelines describe the magazine's contents (true stories, no fiction, and vintage photographs that "bring back the good times" for its readers, and no advertising), its "relaxed and conversational style," and its seven-hundred-word limit on the length of stories. The guidelines tell you exactly how to submit material, including specifications for photographs, and how much you are likely to be paid: fifty dollars and a Classic Red '57 Chevy replica car bank for a feature, or for shorter pieces just the bank, identifying the writer as a "*Reminisce* Staffer."

A great many magazines offer similarly helpful and extensive writers' guidelines on their Web sites.

With the guidelines of a dozen target magazines in hand, you are ready to send out query letters.

Choosing a book publisher is not so different from choosing magazines to submit your work to.

Just as there are several categories of magazines, there are four kinds of book publishers. Most writers will want to focus on the first two:

1. Trade or commercial publishers—the equivalent of mass circulation magazines—publish books of general interest. They sell a relatively large number of copies of each book, and they usually pay authors an advance and royalties on copies sold.

2. Specialized publishers, including university presses and religious and scientific houses, sell fewer copies. Only the most successful authors receive very much income.

Two other kinds of book publishers are of limited interest to most writers:

3. Textbook publishers generally commission their writers to write books tailored to a curriculum and are not likely to consider unsolicited submissions.

4. Vanity presses require the author to pay the cost of publication and do not certify the value of the manuscripts they publish. We say more about vanity presses and self-publishing in the next chapter.

A *trade publisher* will distribute the book widely, mainly through bookstores, and often at a price that the common reader can afford. Some trade publishers have paperback lines in which trade books reach an even wider audience at even lower prices.

A few authors become famous and wealthy by publishing with trade publishers. Trade publishers are businesses, after all, but that also means that they are likely to be more interested in the bottom line than in the technical value of a specialized book. The trade publisher's editors have to work fast and may not pay careful attention to details. If the book is not wildly successful, it may remain in print—that is, available from the publisher—for only one six-month publishing season.

A *specialized publisher* will make your book available to readers worldwide, especially to those who care the most about your subject, rather than the kind of mass readership that leads to fame and wealth. Its marketing will probably be vigorous, but it will be tailored to a specialized readership that can be reached by direct mail, book reviews, and related publicity. Its books are a little less likely to be found in general interest bookstores, although the big chains—Borders and Barnes and Noble—stock a gratifying array of specialized books.

For its smaller market, a specialized publisher will print a much smaller pressrun than a trade publisher would do, and, lacking the economy of scale of a large pressrun, will set a higher retail price.

The specialized publisher's editors are more likely to care about your subject itself and are likely to devote more effort to getting everything right. The publishing schedule will probably be significantly slower than a trade publisher's. If it is a nonprofit publisher, your book can remain in print and available for years, even for decades.

Choosing a book publisher, as with a magazine, begins with your own reading. Pull related books off your own bookshelves or the shelves of a public library and stack them by publisher. Note the publisher's name and address on the copyright page. Search through the preface and acknowledgments for the names of the author's editor and agent. Choose the three or four publishers of the most recent books in your own library that are most closely related to your own manuscript.

As you read the *New York Times Book Review* on Sunday morning, the *New York Review of Books*, and the book reviews in your favorite magazines, note the names of the publishers in the reviews as well as the ads.

At the library you can find further information in reference books such as *Writer's Market*. These books focus on publishers that pay their writers and tend to ignore the vast sea of noncommercial publishers where your book might most appropriately come to harbor.

From your own computer, searching by subject, you can also mine many libraries' electronic card catalogs, Amazon.com, and other electronic resources for the names of appropriate publishers.

Book publishing houses are regularly bought and sold, conglomerated and dissolved. Book editors move from house to house. The telephone directory in the current volume of *Literary Market Place* at the library will help you locate what has become of the publisher and editor of your favorite books. It will also help you find agents' addresses and where your favorite author's editor has landed.

36   Self-Publishing, Electronic Publishing, and Vanity Publishing

There are many good reasons for wanting a professional publisher to publish your work. An editor's selecting it attests to its value. A professional knows how to prepare the book for publication, make copies, store and distribute them, market the book, and account for costs and income. A commercial publisher can put your book in the hands of thousands or even millions of readers.

But the path to acceptance, for most writers, is paved with rejection, and finding a publisher can be fraught with anxiety and questions about self-worth.

As well, seeking a match with an editor takes time. Simply finding a publisher can take months or years. And, after the publishing clock starts, the work of editing, design, printing, and marketing will total six months to two years.

Some writers choose self-publishing as a way of making a living. Writers who address a niche readership may find that they can sell their books without using the elaborate machinery of a professional publishing house. If they've succeeded at other businesses or are willing to learn, they may be able to make self-publishing a success, too.

If speed is important to you, or if you don't want to face rejection, or if you want to learn a new business, and if you are willing to handle all the elements of publication yourself, you can publish your work yourself or consider electronic publishing.

Self-publishing or e-publishing can be fast, if you know what you are doing or can find expert help. Even so, it is a lot of work, and before you turn away from the path of seeking professional publication, you may wish to think through why you are going it on your own. If you can answer *yes* to the following questions, self-publishing may be the answer to your dreams.

Are you impatient by nature?

Can you afford the expense (or the loss, if you decide to self-publish as a business)?

Can you identify your readership by name (daughter Katherine, grandson Bennett) or are you eager to spend the time and energy to find your readership? If you only want to publish a few copies to give to your immediate family, if you don't care whether your book is distributed widely, or if you enjoy selling door to door, then self-publishing may be your ticket.

One Tucsonan, recently retired from owning book and music stores, has self-published ten thousand copies of a little book of his own ideas about how to live well. He gives his book away, and even handing out free copies turns out to be hard work not much different from selling.

Do you have a big garage? Big enough to hold, for many years, the pallets of books you will have had printed but not sold or given away?

Can you dispense with the validation of professional publication? Common readers look to the reputation of the publisher to tell them whether your book merits attention. Scholars and scientists rely upon other scholars' endorsement or peer review of the scholarship in specialized journals such as *Science* and *Nature* and in books published by university presses. University professors need peer-reviewed publication for promotion and tenure. For these readers and writers, self-publication just won't do. But you may not need this sort of validation.

Will your spouse or partner support this venture? Or will the time and expense be a source of friction?

If the answers are *yes*, then self-publishing may be for you.

Self-Publishing Success Stories

Doctor Death. Ken Iserson, MD, a professor of emergency medicine and bioethics at the University of Arizona, wrote, and he and his wife published, a guide to getting into residency programs for newly minted MDS. It's not merely a book that people want. It's a book that new MDS—desperate to complete their training, go into practice, and pay off their college loans—need. It's also about a topic that changes frequently, so Dr. and Mrs. Iserson regularly publish revised editions themselves. Every year the book has a fresh market of new MDS, and each market needs the newest edition.

But the Isersons had more than simply one book with a ready market. They also had skills to bring to the job. Dr. Iserson holds an MBA as well as an MD, and his wife is an editor and a CPA. (If you decide to self-publish and lack Mrs. Iserson's skills, you need to learn to keep accounts well enough to satisfy yourself, or avoid accounting altogether by giving your book away, or if income taxes are not a consideration, reconcile yourself to keeping sloppy accounts or none at all.)

The Isersons had set out not merely to publish one book but to start a publishing house. So they engaged as an adviser Dan Poynter, a Californian who has built a career writing books, teaching seminars, and consulting about self-publishing.

Next, Dr. Iserson wrote, and the Isersons published, *Dust to Dust*, a book about exactly what happens to your body when you die. It's a topic of not merely ghoulish interest—it's critically important to the system of organ and tissue donations. The first edition sold more than forty thousand copies in hardback, and within a couple of years new scientific discoveries justified publishing a revised edition.

Their course was set, and the Isersons are publishing one or more new books per year, all tightly focused on topics of broad medical interest.

Ken Iserson, MD, has become a brand name in two markets: He is unabashedly the Number One Residency Guru worldwide, and among organ donor specialists he is known as Doctor Death.

Hank the Cowdog. John Erickson presents a longer, more grueling story of the path to success in self-publishing.

With a degree from the University of Texas, and following a disillusioning run at Harvard Divinity School, John returned to the Texas Panhandle to write. He supported his family working as a cowboy and a carpenter, rising long before dawn to write for four hours every morning out in the barn. Every morning. For more than twenty-five years.

Professional publishers published John's first three books, all arising from his own life as a Panhandle cowboy, and then John set out on his own.

John began writing detective stories for children about the adventures of Hank the Cowdog, chief of ranch security. To keep control of the books and the income, John published the first book himself and then hit the road with his banjo and a truckload of books and sang and told stories and peddled books in classrooms and everywhere he could find children to sing and talk to in the little towns of West Texas, the Oklahoma Panhandle, and eastern New Mexico.

John kept on writing and publishing and peddling Hank the Cowdog books and tapes, and finally commercial publishers got interested in taking Hank on. As of the year 2000, a division of the paperback giant Viking Penguin had thirty-nine Hank books in print, the fortieth was in the pipeline, and John had finished the manuscript for number forty-one. John says that Hank keeps leading him to stories to write.

John Erickson stands six foot two. He wears a big hat and speaks with a laconic Texas accent. He looks and acts authentically like the writer who lives in the world of Hank the Cowdog. And that's branding.

One professional poet, in addition to the poems and books he places with professional publishers, has published a few books on his own over the years, partly for fun, partly because they don't quite fit the niche of other publishers. He enjoys the work of selection and the craft of seeing the books through the press, and he seems to have only modest expectations about reaching a wide readership.

Another professional writer, the poet Coleman Barks, having established a huge national audience for his translations of the Sufi poet Rumi, was able to found his own publishing house, Maypop Press, through which to distribute his work.

A more customary kind of self-publisher was the late Hannah Cook Westley, who did her self-publishing with unusual determination and good taste. After publishing her mother's memories, which she recorded on regular visits to her mother in a nursing home, Hannah decided to publish her own memoirs. With admirable restraint, she took up only her first twenty-one years. The teacher of a class on writing memoirs gave her an invaluable tip: be confident about your own memories and don't let anyone else talk you out of them. As Hannah said in her book, "All of the places and events in this book are true and unaltered from my memory of them. If anyone reading this has a different memory of this material, it is their memory."

Hannah's memoir is a short book, at only 110 pages, which made it easier to publish and quicker to read, and she sold it as opportunity arose for ten dollars, autographed. To her good fortune, Hannah's son was a graphic designer. Using a Macintosh computer and a copy shop, Hannah said, he "took all my pages and my distressed photographs and gave them a professional tune-up before printing the book." Hannah's memoir is charming and witty and interesting even to people who are not related to her, partly because of her son's attractive and unpretentious design.

Most self-publishers will find that using a copy shop, as Hannah Westley did, is the readiest means of duplicating a few copies of a short book. A local job printer may offer higher quality but probably at a much steeper price. The specialized book manufacturers that print and bind books for commercial publishers offer the top of the line in quality. But self-publishers may find it awkward to work with book manufacturers—their plants are not likely to be just around the corner, and they are set up to do business with established accounts, not with single-book clients.

It's difficult, too, for a self-publisher to get a single book into the national channels of distribution. Even a local bookstore is unlikely to want to, or be able to, distribute a self-published book very successfully, unless the subject of the book holds great interest for the store's customers, or the book is unusually attractive. Dutch Salmon of Silver City, New Mexico, published such a book that he had written about canoeing the Gila River. Salmon's book tells an intriguing southwestern story, and he is an engaging guy who, by persistence, persuaded regional bookstores and distributors to carry his book. They were able to sell it. As Salmon gained experience, he began publishing books by other writers and eventually succeeded as a small regional publisher.

The best avenues of distribution for a self-publisher are probably

— sending and, especially, resending postcards, via direct mail, to lists of friends, relatives, colleagues, and people who might be interested

— sending news releases to an appropriate list of newspapers, magazines, newsletters, and other media

— putting up a Web site and getting the book listed by Amazon.com

— selling books directly at the writer's and/or publisher's speaking engagements.

To succeed in all these media, the writer needs to employ pleasant, calm persistence.

Vanity Publishing

Rather than publishing your book yourself, you can also avoid the process of editorial selection by engaging a subsidy publisher or vanity press (the name means what it says) to put your book in print. You shouldn't have high expectations. What a vanity press will do for you is commonly quite modest, and the reputable ones will spell it out exactly.

The vanity press's basic criterion in selecting manuscripts to publish is whether or not your check bounces. The process is likely to go slowly, and the bill for their services can be shockingly high, but probably not so much more than you would have spent, a thousand bucks here, a thousand bucks there, publishing the book yourself, and a lot less than people spend on other hobbies—collecting art, say, or yachting.

If you are a poet, you may have run across vanity presses that publish poetry anthologies. For a fee, they offer a way of getting your poems into print.

Electronic Publishing

Electronic publishing, or e-pub, generally means making a book widely available on the Internet. E-pub is still new, the dust has not yet settled, and there are many possible variations.

E-publishing works for a piece of writing of any length, from a poem to an encyclopedia.

With e-publishing, you don't have to make multiple copies of your book, article, or poem, and it can be instantly available to millions of people worldwide.

One variation combines features of vanity publishing and self-publishing. For a fairly modest fee, the e-publisher will post your book on the Internet and list it in its catalog and ads. Readers can read the book on-screen, download it, or order a printed copy.

But e-publishing only takes the place of paper, printing, binding, and distribution. It doesn't eliminate the need for editors and designers (even if the editor and designer is you) and marketing. Whether you write a poem, an article, a book, or an evanescent stream of bits and bytes, people have to hear about it, decide they want to read it, and know how to get it.

You still have to do the writer's work of marketing and promotion, and e-pub can come into play there, too, if you decide to get up your own Web site to promote your work.

When you publish on the Web, you enter a huge, floating, chaotic mass of human expression, where factual and ethical rigor are up for grabs, like the mass of private correspondence and popular hand-bills, broadsides, ballads, and street-corner harangues that flooded the English-speaking world during the rise, in the nineteenth century, of literacy, democracy, and printing technology.

37 A Few Observations about Copyright

Copyright is a law that protects the right of writers and other artists to benefit from the fruits of their labor. Broadly, copyright is the *right to sell copies* of their work.

Copyright protects all kinds of creative work—paintings, photographs, architectural drawings, musical compositions, choreography, and even computer code.

Ever since the first United States copyright statute was enacted in 1790, copyright has encouraged artists and writers to produce informative and inspiring work and to make it widely available. It does that by protecting the livelihood of individual workers, individual artists.

The idea of copyright is simple and straightforward, but in practice copyright law is complicated and ambiguous, too.

The best source of information is the U.S. Copyright Public Information Office. The phone number is (202) 707–5959, and knowledgeable people are waiting to take your call. The U.S. Copyright Office also has a generally informative Web site, www.loc.gov/copyright.

For a practical understanding of copyright, we refer you to William S. Strong's plainspoken manual addressed expressly to writers and artists, entitled *The Copyright Book: A Practical Guide.*

As well, any lawyer can refer you to an attorney specializing in copyright. Large general practice law firms sometimes have a copyright specialist among their partners.

Perhaps we would be wisest just to stop right there, but we can't resist offering a few observations.

However noble the impulse behind copyright protection, in the digital age writers are little fish in a big copyright pond. Large corporations—which own copyrights to an array of inventions, from computer programs to Mickey Mouse—have asserted control over the drafting of copyright law. Other large institutions, such as university libraries, also take an active interest.

Still, copyright helps individual writers protect their own rights in what they have written. It protects you, and it protects the writers you want to quote.

In a nutshell, if I want to copy and sell something that you wrote, or a quotation from your work, I need to obtain your permission. And I need to pay you if you charge a fee for granting permission.

Copyright is not just one thing. It's a bundle of five rights—the right to

reproduce a work

distribute copies to the public

make derivative works, such as adaptations and books on tape

perform the work, and

display it publicly.

Different artists find different rights important. Novelists "distribute copies." Playwrights "perform." Painters "display publicly." (Usually, of course, it's a publisher who distributes copies of the novel, a theater company that performs the play, and a gallery that displays the paintings—with the artist's permission.)

Expression, originality, and *fixation* are the keys to copyright protection. That is, you can copyright only the particular way you have *expressed* an *original* production of your mind, *fixed* in tangible form, whether with pen on paper or on a computer disk. Copyright protects things, not ideas. That is, it protects the particular way you have expressed your ideas in tangible form, not what's in your head.

Copyright law does not protect your mere idea for a novel, no matter how original. It only comes into force at the moment you set pen to paper. (Some works that are not expressed in fixed form, such as pantomime, which exists only in performance, can be protected by common law copyright, but that does not affect you as a writer.)

To obtain copyright protection, you only need to start writing. If you mean to distribute a few copies, such as photocopies at a conference, it is a good idea to signal your ownership by putting "Copyright (c) [year and your name go here], All Rights Reserved," on the first page.

Careful writers register the complete manuscript for a book that they are planning to submit for publication, and journalists register all the pieces they've published in a year in one fell swoop. That way, people who want permission to reprint them can find the author's address through the U.S. Copyright Office.

You needn't even register your unpublished writing with the U.S. Copyright Office to gain copyright protection. However, to bring suit to enforce your copyright you must have registered it. Registration is a fairly simple process. You can obtain the forms from the U.S. Copyright Office Web site, www.loc.gov/copyright.

Professional writers don't usually register their notes, which comprise ideas and facts more than the expression—the final string of words—used in the work. Nor do they usually register unpublished manuscripts that they're not showing to anyone else.

The plots of works of fiction are protected, and so are fictional characters, but more as a matter of ordinary property law than copyright.

After a publisher accepts your manuscript for publication, typically the publisher handles registering it for copyright.

Copyright protects your work until seventy years after your death. Everything any American has written since 1978 has that protection under the Copyright Act of 1976. After the term expires, your writing falls into the public domain and anybody can use it with impunity. (The span of copyright is different for the works created before 1978 that you may wish to quote in your own books and articles.)

Copyright offers endless learning, befuddling, and arguing opportunities.

We've listed copyright references under Further Reading in the back of the book, including complete addresses for the U.S. Copyright Office, which is the authoritative source of copyright information.

38

There are two sides to copyright law—protecting your property and protecting the property of others.

In protecting the property of others, copyright law tells you not to quote or copy someone else's writing without his or her permission.

But unlike other laws, copyright law has a doctrine called fair use.

The idea of fair use is quite lofty. It's meant to foster the intellectual life of the nation by encouraging writers to test their ideas against those of others. To do that, writers need to be able to quote other writers freely and accurately.

Fair use simply permits you to copy—in a sense, to borrow—other people's writing, without obtaining their permission, for purposes of scholarship and criticism.

But there has to be a limit to how much you can copy without permission. Otherwise, your use is not fair.

If you infringe someone else's copyright, you have deprived that person of an opportunity, however slight, to profit financially from his or her work.

If you quote extensively from another person's work, people might use your book or article instead of purchasing the source you are quoting. The other writer then loses the opportunity to earn royalties on that lost sale, and that's not fair.

How can you tell when a use is fair? The law doesn't say. But courts use five criteria to define fair use.

The first criterion is quantitative: Courts are more likely to consider your quotation fair use if it does not represent (a) a *large* part or (b) a *substantial* part of the original.

For example, a quotation one page long is usually a *large* part of any piece of writing and surely would not be fair use—you would need to obtain the writer's permission to use it.

And four lines of a seven-line poem would be a *substantial* part of that poem (even though it wouldn't add up to a *large* amount of poetry), and you would need to obtain the poet's permission to quote.

Of course, a quotation from a book of prose may be both large and substantial: five pages lifted from a book of two hundred pages, say, would require permission.

Unfortunately, the copyright law does not define either *large* or *substantial*. It leaves it to the courts to decide, in each case, how much is too much.

The second criterion is even vaguer: Courts are more likely to consider your quotation fair use if your purpose in writing your article or book is nonprofit and educational rather than commercial—as if writers didn't want to earn a living by conveying useful information.

The *third* criterion splits an even finer hair: It's more likely to be fair use if the work you are quoting, rather than being largely literary (a poem or short story, for example), is informational.

The *fourth* criterion follows up on the second criterion by getting down to money: Your quotation is more likely to be fair use if it will not undermine the financial value of the work you are quoting. How much income is the copyright owner losing by your quoting the work without permission? The answer is uncertain at best, and resolving uncertainty can be expensive if you retain a lawyer to do it.

Fortunately, the *fifth* criterion is a pretty easy yes or no: Your quotation is more likely to be fair use if you are quoting a source that has been published (a book or magazine article, for example) rather than unpublished (a private letter you found in an archive, say). If you have written an article for publication in which you quote an unpublished source, you will need permission to quote from it.

Despite the vagueness of the five criteria, writers need to use fair use bravely to keep the right from withering away. But they also need to use it fairly.

In quoting others, the best practice is:

1. Quote others accurately, whether the quote is long or short. That's not only a matter of copyright, it's a responsibility, an obligation, a courtesy to your readers and to the original writer.

2. Put the quote in quotation marks (or indent it as a block, or "extract") so you won't be taking credit for something someone else wrote.

3. Cite the original source—writer, place of publication, date of publication or copyright date, page number—exactly. Give the original writer credit.

4. In deciding how extensive a quotation you can use, ask yourself, Am I using it as an example, or is it taking the place of writing I can do myself?

5. Then decide whether it's fair use or a quotation for which you must seek permission.

No quantitative formula will tell you whether the use you intend is fair. Nevertheless, here are our rules of thumb, not to be construed as a legal opinion:

> If you quote more than five lines of a poem, or 10 percent of a short poem, obtain permission.
>
> If you quote more than fifty continuous *words* of a work of prose, or if your article, chapter, or entire book is freckled with quotes from a single source, obtain permission.
>
> Don't quote the lyrics of any song in copyright. The music guys are aggressive, expensive, and inflexible—think "pit bulls"—and it's not worth fighting them.
>
> If your publisher's editor questions whether any quotation is fair use, rewrite or omit it without a moment's hesitation.
>
> Obtain other writers' permission before quoting them extensively.

The safest practice, of course, is to quote other writers as little as possible and to put everything in your own words. Come to think of it, why would you ever have wanted to use somebody else's words and deprive yourself of a writing opportunity?

Anyway, requesting permissions is a pain in the neck.

39   Obtaining Permission to Quote

Obtaining permissions is a pain in the neck, and it follows that the more permissions you have to obtain, the greater the pain.
For one thing, you have to wait until the last minute.

> You can't request permissions until you know what you want to quote, and you won't know that until you've finished writing the piece.

> You can't request permissions until your work is accepted for publication, because you need to say in your permission requests who will publish your book or article.

> And, after your book is well into production and a publication date is set, the publisher's editor may spot a quotation for which you need to obtain permission.

The exchange of correspondence to obtain permission can be maddeningly slow, just when you want things to go fast.

Each publisher or writer or writer's agent may receive hundreds or thousands of permission requests a week. Your request has to take its place in queue, and a multimillion-dollar offer for movie rights will probably jump the line ahead of your modest request for permission to quote.

Adding to the agony, each writer and each publisher is free to set his or her own permission fees. Depending upon the nature of the material you want to quote, and the extent and proposed use of the quote, the fee may vary from twenty dollars to several thousand.

Not only that, the writer or publisher is not obliged to grant you permission. They're not likely to refuse, but they get to decide, and there's nothing you can do about it.

To seek permission to quote, you write to the rights and permissions department of the magazine or book publisher that published the work you wish to quote.

Publishers go out of business and magazines change their names, so you may have to write several letters to get your request to the right person.

To find the correct address, you use the masthead of the magazine, the copyright page (reverse of the title page) of a book, a library reference book such as *Literary Market Place*, or the publisher's Web site.

Also, the United States Copyright Office can help you find the proprietor of the rights in question, and an outfit called the Copyright Clearance Center can also facilitate requests for permission to use material controlled by many publishers.

Your request letter is simple and straightforward. In a letter addressed to the attention of the rights and permissions department of the publisher, on your letterhead, you say simply something like this:

Dear [editor's name]:
I am writing to request permission to quote [amount of text: three hundred words, five lines, whatever] from [author, title, place of publication, copyright date] in all printings and editions of my forthcoming book, [title of your book].

My book will be published in [specify whether hardback or paperback] by [name of publisher] in an edition of [specify approximate initial pressrun] in [season or month of publication]. It is a [some phrase to indicate the size and nature of the intended readership: scholarly book, educational text, article of general interest, memoir published for the members of my local engineering society].

I have enclosed photocopies of the passages I wish to quote, with page citations and word count indicated.

I will be happy to answer any questions you may have about this request. May I please hear from you soon?

Sincerely yours,
[your signature]

From the publication date you have specified for your book, the publisher can tell how urgent your request is.

Be sure to indicate your telephone number, e-mail address, and fax number, if you have one, so that the publisher can respond quickly and efficiently.

The publisher may have a form for you to fill out and return either by mail or electronically.

Your own publisher will offer advice and may be able to provide sample permission request letters. You may even have been able to negotiate a contract by which your publisher agrees to handle permission requests.

Publishers' rights departments make their money from big movie, paperback, and foreign rights deals, not from requests for permission to quote. This has three implications for you. First, they probably won't charge you an exorbitant fee. Second, the person handling low-income permission requests such as yours may be new at the business, certainly will be underpaid, and merits your compassion. Third, in the press of thousands of requests, they may not respond to your request as fast as you could wish.

We counsel patience. You can always repeat your request, but it is a good idea to do so courteously. If in your second letter you ask politely for a reply by a certain date, you've laid the groundwork for a follow-up request.

And if the permission fee does seem exorbitant, you can make a reasoned, factual case (showing for example that your book or article is scholarly and noncommercial) asking the publisher or author to reconsider, and you may get a reduced rate.

40 Protecting Your Copyright

Using someone else's copyright material without permission is called copyright infringement.

If someone infringes your copyright and you don't call them on it, in effect you've forfeited your copyright.

How can you catch the culprit? Some writers systematically read new publications and scan Web sites in their specialties, looking for writers who may have unfairly published or quoted from their work without permission. Other writers in your specialty may tell you if somebody appears to be blatantly violating your copyright—although even your best pals don't know your work as well as you do. Or you may run across infringement by blind luck.

If you suspect that someone has infringed your copyright, your first step is to inspect the book or article in question as objectively as you can. Copyright protects expression—not your ideas nor the facts you report—and the other work is infringement only if it meets three tests:

1. It uses your writing word for word.

2. You did not grant permission.

3. It's not fair use.

(You can sometimes make a case for infringement even if the passage does not copy your work word for word but demonstrates such "substantial similarity" as to infringe the underlying copyright in your work. Lawyers call this "nonverbatim copying.")

If, on calm reflection, you believe that the passage does indeed infringe your copyright, your second step can range from a polite letter requesting a correction in the next issue of a magazine, to a threat, on your lawyer's letterhead, to sue the infringer back into the Stone Age.

Either the infringer settles out of court or not.

41 Conveying Rights: Contracts

In essence, a publishing contract expresses the terms under which the author is conveying rights to the publisher. (Your publishing contract governs the terms even if the copyright is registered in your name.)

You can convey all or part of the copyright in your work to the publisher, and you can negotiate the terms of conveying it.

For instance, you can sell or give a magazine the right to publish one of your poems, reserving all other rights, including the right to publish the poem later in a collection of your own work.

You can convey the paperback rights in your published work to a paperback publisher, and you can specify that the rights revert to you after a period of time—five years, say—giving the publisher enough time to sell out its edition.

You can convey rights exclusively or nonexclusively. One magazine may want the exclusive right to publish a chapter from your forthcoming book. On the other hand, many publishers have obtained the nonexclusive right to publish Carl Sandburg's little poem "Fog" in their textbooks.

And the rights are not gone for good. Even if the copyright is in the publisher's name, you can still control most of the rights, depending upon the wording of your contract. As well, you and your heirs have the statutory right to terminate the contract thirty-five years after you granted the rights, or forty years after first publication.

The contract or agreement itself, which the publisher will send you upon accepting your work for publication, can be anything from a simple one-paragraph letter to a book contract running eight to ten single-spaced pages.

An agreement with a magazine tends to be fairly simple. The magazine will usually want only "first serial rights"—the right of the magazine to publish the piece for the first time. The magazine will take copyright in its name and will probably revert all other rights to you, although it should spell out whether it wants to post your work online as well. For maximum international protection of your copyright, you should have the copyright notice in your own name, if possible. Most magazines won't go for this, but as we mentioned in our copyright chapter, you can always later register all your newspaper and magazine work for a twelve-month period, in your own name, in a single application.

A contract with a book publisher may run to several pages and may address many details—deadlines, schedule of royalty payments, and other matters that may never have occurred to you. Negotiating a contract with a book publisher is where a good agent, if you have one, will come in handy.

Publishing is a partnership between writer and publisher, and the contract expresses the terms of that partnership. Even so, the contract is the publisher's form, written to favor the publisher's interests. An agent will recognize from experience which clauses can remain as written and which ones should be changed to improve the lot of the author.

Members of the Authors' Guild have access to the Guild's contract form, written to favor the writer. The Guild will also provide advice about a particular contract.

If you are negotiating the contract yourself, you will find that it is written in legalese. There's no point in asking the publisher to rewrite it in finely wrought literary English, but otherwise you can ask any questions about it that you wish, especially about the rights conveyed.

Somewhere the contract will specify the transfer of rights. Some book publishers may want only particular rights of publication. More commonly, a book publisher will ask you to convey all the rights listed in our copyright chapter—the rights to reproduce, distribute copies, make derivative works, perform, and display the work publicly. That is, the publisher will ask you to transfer your copyright.

You don't have to do it.

If you convey all the rights, the publisher's rights and permissions department will handle the tedium of rights negotiations, but you'll only get a percentage of the income—maybe 50 percent on most rights and 75 percent on the higher-ticket items such as paperback and movie rights.

By retaining as many of the rights as possible and signing an agreement with the Copyright Clearance Center to handle rights, you can hold onto a much larger percentage of the income.

You want to be sure that the contract takes specific account of electronic rights, assigning them either to you or to the publisher.

Your book contract should also have a clause that says that any rights not assigned in the contract belong to the author, not one that says that they belong to the publisher.

Although you can negotiate what rights you convey to the publisher, there's no point in being contentious about things that are unlikely to come to pass. Is someone really going to produce a Broadway musical based on your botany of southern Ohio?

Contracts tend to focus on who gets the money, but for most writers the money from any one article or book doesn't actually amount to much, only enough to consider deducting some expenses on your income tax, or to show your friends and family that writing is not just a hobby.

Every contract needs an ironclad termination clause. You want to be able to sell and resell the rights in your work, so you need to specify that rights revert to you at some point.

You might specify cancellation of the contract and a reversion of rights if the publisher does not publish the book by a certain date. That protects your copyright from an honest publisher who lacks the will, skill, or money to publish on schedule, or from a vanity publisher who takes your money and intentionally sits on your manuscript.

Book contracts commonly specify reversion of rights to the author if a book goes out of print in all editions. In that case, you want the burden of proof to fall on the publisher, not on you—the publisher should have to prove that the book is in print, rather than your proving that it is not.

Better, you might specify reversion of rights ten or twenty years after publication. That gives the publisher enough time to make some money and gives you a concrete date on which you can peddle the book, if it still has some life in it, to another publisher.

Besides spelling out the tiny amount of money most writers will make, a book contract also mentions that writers actually assume considerable financial risks that the publisher seeks to duck. A book contract will almost surely include a "hold harmless" clause in which you agree to hold the publisher harmless from suits for libel and other damages. You can negotiate to reduce the effect of this clause by limiting the amount of damages you will pay, but even if the clause is absent anybody can sue anybody else.

Effective or not, the "hold harmless" clause brings home this lesson: you should conscientiously avoid harming other people in your book, either by infringing their copyright, by libeling them, or by invading their privacy.

42 Libel and Invasion of Privacy

Libel

Libel is injury to a living person's reputation.

Most people want to enjoy a good reputation.

Libel isn't a matter of merely embarrassing someone.

Libel is a matter of injuring a living person. (You can't injure or libel a dead person—or, as lawyers put it, there is no defamation of the dead.)

Most of us depend on our reputation to make a living, and an injury to our reputation could be ruinous financially.

If you injure a person's reputation for living within the law or for moral rectitude, for example—if you say that they deal dishonestly with customers or that they don't treat their families well—you may be accused of libel.

And if you accuse a person of a crime of which she or he has not been convicted; if you make a libelous charge against a group to which that person belongs; or if you call a person a Nazi or a Communist, you have committed libel on the face of it.

If you are a reporter or a writer of nonfiction books, you have an obligation to tell your readers what you find, truthfully. You may find that the truth imperils some living person's reputation.

How can you avoid libel? The first line of defense in court is to prove that what you have written is true. The best defense is to have backup for every statement you make. That's one of many reasons to confirm and verify the facts in your story or book and even to research the other side of the story.

If you are lucky enough to be published by the *New Yorker*, the magazine's famous fact-checkers may provide some solace by double-checking the quotations and facts in your article, but even they don't let you off the hook.

The Golden Rule is a good test: Do unto others what you would have them do unto you. If John Jones had written about you what you have just written about John Jones, would you consider your reputation damaged? If so, you'd better be extra sure that you can back up what you have written.

Nor is it good enough to say that you quoted accurately a reliable source who made the charge against the other person. You must be able to demonstrate that what your source said is true. A lie, even if you quote it word for word, is still a lie.

In most states, pleading that you made an honest mistake won't win you many points, either. (Libel is a matter of state law, not federal law, and mostly case law at that, so it varies from state to state.) In New York, private figures have to prove malice and "grossly irresponsible" disregard for the truth in order to sue for libel. But people in other states have successfully sued for libel on the basis of falsehoods arising from mere negligence.

In other words, courts are requiring writers to work ever more conscientiously to get their facts straight.

It helps if you never meant to hurt the guy. A mitigating courtroom defense is to show that you meant no malice. Still, you have to ask whether you really want to wind up in court.

Because libel arises almost entirely in civil law, your legal risk is largely financial. (Criminal libel is an extremely small risk. It would come into play if you wrote something libelous that resulted in a breach of the peace—for instance, a riot in the streets.)

The cost of losing a libel suit can vary. In establishing damages, a court or a jury may assess the actual harm that the libel has done. Imagine that something you wrote has caused a carpenter to lose his livelihood, neighbors to shun a housewife leading to years of psychiatric treatment, or patients to abandon a doctor. The damages can be steep.

Even if his or her publisher shares the risk and the cost, a sensible writer is not likely to relish being the defendant in a libel suit.

Writers reporting on public life—such as reporters for daily newspapers—enjoy one special protection from libel suits.

Public officials have what is called absolute privilege. They can say false, malicious, and damaging things in court, in the legislature, and in other official proceedings free of any danger of being sued for libel. Most public records may also report such statements without being libelous.

Reporters, by extension, have qualified privilege. That is, they can report what public officials say (or public documents report) under absolute privilege without committing libel, so long as what they write is full, fair, accurate, and impartial. Even then, to win a libel case a public figure must prove the statements are false (rather than the reporter's proving they're true), and the public figure must prove actual malice, which is difficult to prove.

But the courts are narrowing their definition of public person or official, reducing the number of people you can comment on without risking libel. And, because courts are moving away from the standard of "reckless disregard for truth" to simple negligence, citizens' right to sue for libel is being broadened while the writer's right to comment is being narrowed.

Invasion of Privacy

We all have a perfect right to our privacy, to live a private life out of the public eye. Based on that premise, the right of privacy enjoys a robust life in the courts.

But unless your article or book sordidly, crudely, ruthlessly exploits the misfortunes or personal affairs of private citizens who have not been involved in some event that would thrust them into public view, invasion of privacy is unlikely to arise.

SECTION NINE

Acknowledgments and Further Reading

43 Acknowledgments

With all our hearts we thank our friends who have read and commented on this book at many stages of its writing. We are grateful for their encouraging words.

Ted thanks his teachers, the late Mary McNally, Will Jumper, and Karl Shapiro, from whom he learned to write.

Steve thanks Rev. Nancy Roemheld, Kathy Norgard, Bill Bemis, Norm Epstein, Carol Schaefer, Charles Gillespie, Gretchen Nielsen, Ken Kennon, Tom Miller, Jay Rochlin, Ana Luisa Terrazas, Judith Allen, and above all his patient, percipient, and supportive wife and son, Barbara Kremer and Joseph Cox.

Dozens of "how to write" books are published every year. Here are a few that we have quoted or cited, and a few others that you might find encouraging and useful.

Aronie, Nancy Slonim. *Writing from the Heart: Tapping the Power of Your Inner Voice.* New York: Hyperion, 1998.

Atchity, Kenneth. *A Writer's Time: A Guide to the Creative Process from Vision through Revision.* New York: W. W. Norton, 1986. Atchity works through a schedule, an agenda, for writing a book, including time for vacations between drafts.

Ballenger, Bruce, and Barry Lane. *Discovering the Writer Within: 40 Days to More Imaginative Writing.* Cincinnati: Writer's Digest Books, 1989. Full of imperatives: "Make a list of every person you've known." Not a bad idea, as a jump start.

Boice, Robert. "Strategies for Enhancing Scholarly Productivity." In *Writing and Publishing for Academic Authors,* edited by Joseph M. Moxley and Todd Taylor. 2nd ed. Lanham MD: Rowman and Littlefield, 1997.

Cox, Stephen. "How to Write History," *Annals of Iowa* 49, nos. 3, 4 (Winter/Spring 1988): 261–67.

Goldberg, Natalie. *Writing Down the Bones: Freeing the Writer Within.* Boston: Shambhala, 1986. Zen approach. Writing as practice, i.e., developing a good habit. Choose a topic and write for ten minutes on that topic. Choose a time and write every day at that time for ten minutes. Also author of *Wild Mind: Living the Writer's Life* (New York: Bantam, 1990), about being a professional writer, and *Living Color* (New York: Bantam, 1997). Audios are available of her classes and talks.

Gray, Francine du Plessix. Comments on learning writing from the

poet Charles Olson. Quoted in *Black Mountain: An Exploration in Community*, by Martin Duberman, 376 (New York:
Dutton, 1972).

Hampl, Patricia. *I Could Tell You Stories*. New York: W. W. Norton,
1999. Biography as a literary form.

Kazin, Alfred. *A Walker in the City*. New York: Harcourt, Brace, 1951. A
model recollection of a boyhood. Every American memoirist
can profit from reading it before setting pen to paper or finger
to keyboard.

King, Stephen. *On Writing: A Memoir of the Craft*. New York: Scribner,
2000. A memoir, as the title says, that holds nuggets of advice
for writers of nonfiction as well as fiction.

Lamott, Anne. *Bird by Bird: Some Instructions on Writing and Life*. New
York: Pantheon 1994. A much-beloved how-to-write book,
itself a memoir, aimed toward writing professionally.

Larsen, Michael. *How to Write a Book Proposal*. 3rd ed. Cincinnati:
Writer's Digest Books, 2003.

Le Guin, Ursula K. *Steering the Craft: Exercises and Discussions on Story
Writing for the Lone Navigator or the Mutinous Crew*. Portland
OR: Eighth Mountain Press, 1998. Grew out of classes taught
by a swell writer.

Moxley, Joseph M. *Publish, Don't Perish: The Scholar's Guide to Academic Writing and Publishing*. Foreword by Robert Boice.
Westport CT: Greenwood Press, 1992. A comprehensive how-
to-write book, meant for university professors but full of
useful tips for every beginning writer. The source of our six
ways of outlining in our chapter titled "Getting Organized."

New York Times, "Writers on Writing," an occasional Monday morning
newspaper feature. The whole run can be found on the Web
at www.nytimes.com/arts. Susan Sontag, Barbara Kingsolver,
Elmore Leonard, Kent Haruf, John Updike, E. L., Doctorow,
Ed McBain, Annie Proulx, Jamaica Kincaid, and Saul Bellow
have written pieces for this feature.

Sloane, William. *The Craft of Writing*, edited by Julia H. Sloane. New
York: W. W. Norton, 1979.

Smith, Michael C., and Suzanne Greenberg. *Panning for Gold in the
Kitchen Sink: Everyday Creative Writing*. Chicago: NTC Pub-

lishing Group 1999. Treats the insight, memory, sensations that things around your house can prompt. The stories that an archive of years of old canceled checks can tell. The odor, taste, and feel of iceberg lettuce. The memories and feelings that things trigger and that you can write from and about.

Stanek, Lou Willett. *Writing Your Life: Putting Your Past on Paper.* New York: Avon, 1996. Lots of exercises such as, "Write about the biggest bully you ever encountered." Says that you learn to write by writing.

Strunk, William Jr., and E. B. White. *The Elements of Style.* 3rd ed. New York: Macmillan, 1979.

E. B. White was the editor of the *New Yorker,* which set the standard for American English writing in the 1930s. Through thick and thin, *New Yorker* style has scarcely wavered in the seventy years that the magazine has been published.

William Strunk Jr., of Cornell University, taught English to White and to hundreds of other students early in the twentieth century. Strunk called his manual "the little book." In his edition, E. B. White introduced the foundation of his writing style to the wider world.

Stephen King observes that all you need to know about grammar you can get from Strunk and White and the endpapers of Warriner's (see below).

Ueland, Brenda. *If You Want to Write: A Book about Art, Independence, and Spirit.* New York: Putnam, 1938; reprint, Schubert Club of St. Paul, 1983; paperback, Minneapolis: Gray Wolf, n.d. An inspiring book that grew out of a writing class Ueland taught at the Minneapolis YWCA. It's unpretentious, very practical, very direct, and it's full of citations and quotations of Ueland's own wide and deep reading. Ueland also wrote an autobiography simply entitled *Me* and another very spirited book about writing, *Strength to Your Sword Arm.*

Warriner, John E. *English Composition Grammar: Complete Course.* New York: Harcourt Brace Jovanovich, 1988. Recently, though, Warriner seems to have written many editions of a *Holt Handbook* for Holt, Rinehart, and Winston. (For comment, see Strunk and White.)

Welty, Eudora. *One Writer's Beginnings.* Cambridge MA: Harvard University Press, 1984.

Zinsser, William, ed. *Inventing the Truth: The Art and Craft of Memoir.* Boston: Houghton Mifflin, 1998. Essays by well-known memoirists and writers Russell Baker, Jill Ker Conway, Annie Dillard, Ian Frazier, Henry Louis Gates Jr., Alfred Kazin, Frank McCourt, Toni Morrison, and Eileen Simpson. The essays are gems, the authors' bibliographies at the back of the book are treasure chests, and a person thinking of writing a memoir could do a heck of a lot worse than to spend a few weeks on the front porch reading the books they write about here—Conway's *The Road from Coorain*, Kazin's *A Walker in the City*, McCourt's *Angela's Ashes*, and (although they are novels, not memoirs) Toni Morrison's *Song of Solomon* and *Beloved.*

———. *On Writing Well: An Informal Guide to Writing Nonfiction.* New York: Harper and Row, 1980. A well-known book.

45 Copyright, Libel, and Invasion of Privacy

Abrams, Howard. *The Law of Copyright*. New York: Clark Boardman, 1989.

Authors' Guild Web site, at www.authorsguild.org, offers extremely valuable advice for negotiating a publishing contract and other useful information, but the highly regarded Authors' Guild model contract, written in the author's favor, is not posted, being officially available only to members of the Guild. Membership is open only to professional authors meeting Guild standards of publication.

The Chicago Manual of Style. 15th ed. Chicago: University of Chicago Press, 2003.

Goldstein, Norm, ed. *The Associated Press Stylebook and Libel Manual*. Rev. ed. New York: Addison-Wesley, 1998.

Goldstein, Paul. *Copyright: Principles, Laws, and Practices*. Boston: Little Brown, 1989.

Nimmer, Melville. *Cases and Materials on Copyright*. St. Paul MN: West, 1985.

Patry, William F. *The Fair Use Privilege in Copyright Law*. Washington DC: BNA Books, 1985.

Perle, E. Gabriel, and John Taylor Williams, *Publishing Law Handbook*. 2nd ed. Englewood Cliffs NJ: Prentice-Hall Law and Business Books, 1992.

Sanford, Bruce W. *Libel and Privacy: The Prevention and Defense of Litigation*. Clifton NJ: Law and Business Harcourt Brace Jovanovich, 1985.

———. *Synopsis of the Law of Libel and the Right of Privacy*. Scripps-Howard Newspapers and Scripps-Howard Broadcasting, n.d. Recommended by UPI stylebook for further information.

Strong, William S. *The Copyright Book: A Practical Guide*. 5th ed. Cambridge MA: MIT Press, 1999.

United Press International. *UPI Stylebook: The Authoritative Handbook for Writers, Editors and News Directors*. 3rd ed. Lincolnwood IL: National Textbook Company, 1992.

United States Copyright Office Web site, www.loc.gov/copyright, offers a host of information including its Circular 1, "Copyright Basics"; copyright forms that you can print out or fill out online; and testimony and news of current copyright matters.

The Copyright Office mailing address is:

Register of Copyrights
U.S. Copyright Office
Library of Congress
101 Independence Avenue
Washington DC 20559–6000

The U.S. Copyright Public Information Office telephone number is (202) 707–5959.

Weinstein, David A. *How to Protect Your Creative Work: All You Need to Know about Copyright*. New York: Wiley and Sons, 1987.

University of Nebraska Press

Books by Ted Kooser, Poet Laureate of the United States
and Pulitzer Prize winner:

WRITING BRAVE AND FREE
Encouraging Words for People Who Want to Start Writing
By Ted Kooser and Steve Cox

Writing Brave and Free is a down-to-earth and inspirational guide for anyone
of any age who wishes to write. Organized into forty-five bite-sized chapters,
the book allows aspiring writers to dip in anywhere and learn something of
value, including practical publishing advice rarely found in competing books.

ISBN: 0-8032-2780-9; 978-0-8032-2780-4 (cloth)
      0-8032-7832-2; 978-0-8032-7832-5 (paper)

THE POETRY HOME REPAIR MANUAL
Practical Advice for Beginning Poets

In the pages of *The Poetry Home Repair Manual*, Kooser brings four decades
of experience to bear. Much more than a guidebook to writing and revising
poems, this manual has all the comforts and merits of a long and enlightening
conversation with a wise and patient old friend—a friend who is willing to
share everything he's learned about the art he's spent a lifetime learning to
execute so well.

ISBN: 0-8032-2769-8; 978-0-8032-2769-9 (cloth)

LOCAL WONDERS
Seasons in the Bohemian Alps

"Ted Kooser's *Local Wonders* is the quietest magnificent book I've ever read."
—Jim Harrison, author of *Legends of the Fall*. Ted Kooser describes with
exquisite detail and humor the place he calls home in the rolling hills of
southeastern Nebraska—an area known as the Bohemian Alps. A seer in
the truest sense of the word, Kooser discovers the extraordinary within the
ordinary, the deep beneath the shallow.

ISBN: 0-8032-2751-5; 978-0-8032-2751-4 (cloth)
      0-8032-7811-X; 978-0-8032-7811-0 (paper)

Available wherever books are sold, or call 1-800-755-1105, or order online at
www.unp.unl.edu

When ordering, mention code XK006 to receive a 20% discount.